The power of the
Angels

HINKLER
BOOKS

Author: Adolfo Pérez Agustí
Angel illustrations: Antonio Perera
Editor: Susan Powell
Cover illustration: Trevor Powell, Watermark Creative Pty Ltd
Prepress: Splitting Image
Typesetting: Palmer Higgs
Art direction: Katy Wall
Design: Katy Wall and Silvana Paolini

First published in 2007 by Hinkler Books Pty Ltd
45–55 Fairchild Street,
Heatherton VIC 3202 Australia
www.hinklerbooks.com

Cards and original text: © Editorial LIBSA. Madrid 2005
Design and translation: © Hinkler Books Pty Ltd 2007

10 9 8 7 6 5 4
12 11 10

ISBN 978 1 7415 7417 3

Printed and bound in China

Contents

Introduction

Introduction

A ngels! The existence and role of these celestial beings – mankind's helpers on a divine mission from God – is long recognised in recorded human history. With angels now the focus of renewed interest around the world, this pack of *The Power of the Angels* book and its associated 72 angel cards has been especially developed to show men and women of today how to invite the loving entities into their own lives.

Angels – the word comes from Greek for 'messenger' – are emissaries of God, distinguished by what they do rather than by their external appearance. God created the uncountable numbers of angels in order that they continually adore and worship Him and carry out His will for individuals and for nations on earth.

The Old and the New Testaments of the Bible and the Koran – holy books of Christians, Jews and Muslims – contain many accounts of angelic intervention in human lives, and divine energies akin to angels are part of some other major faiths and appear in holy writings. Our scriptures say that angels are ready and willing to protect, guide and help us – all we need to do is call on them.

The Power of the Angels and its set of beautifully illustrated angel cards are a wonderful means of learning more about individual angels and how and when they can assist in everyday life. You can encourage them to do so through using the cards in various ways or following the many other suggestions for communication and contact that are included in the book.

The first two chapters of the book explain the qualities and attributes of angels, their place in human history from ancient times to the present, and details of rituals, procedures and prayers useful in making angelic connection a part of your life. In this section questions are addressed, issues are discussed and detailed directions are given.

Chapter 3 provides vivid descriptions of the main characteristics of each of the 72 angels in the deck, and instructions and suggestions for ways of dealing and interpreting the cards, including those based on birth dates (for which a chart is given). It is traditionally believed that the angels are organised into hierarchies, headed by the powerful archangels, and the image of each angel in the deck is outlined in a colour that denotes the hierarchy to which it belongs. Other information is provided about the ruling planet of each of these angels, the time of day when they are at their strongest, and reasons for invoking particular angels.

Of recent years, many people around the world have told of their fruitful and reassuring contact with angels in various guises, whether spiritual beings had been called on or not. Chapter 4 contains many first-person accounts of contemporary contact with angels in a surprising range of situations. Perhaps you will soon have your own angel story to tell…

At the end is a useful glossary of wider terms relating to the Christian Church as a context for connecting with angels.

Angelic Beings

There shall no evil befall thee,
neither shall any plague come nigh thy dwelling.
For He shall give His Angels charge over thee,
to keep thee in all thy ways.
(Psalm 91: 10–11)

What are angels?

From the dawn of existence, human beings have believed that they are not alone in the universe. For several thousand years – in churches, synagogues, mosques, temples, at altars and other holy places – people of the major faiths and cultures have worshipped a loving and merciful Creator. At the same time, many have sensed that celestial beings besides God were also looking after them.

Such awareness of 'something else' is not surprising. In their accounts of the invisible, spiritual dimension to our physical and tangible world, the Bible (the holy book of Christians and Jews) and the Koran (the holy book of Islam) speak frequently of God's special messengers, the angels. Some other religions – Hinduism and Buddhism, for example – also recognise the influence of benign spiritual entities. (Non-believers too can be aware of angelic influences, but may refer to fate or chance, guides, masters or archetypes.)

According to the Christian, Jewish and Islamic scriptures, angels are spiritual beings whose role is to carry out the work of the supreme being in His universal mission. Close to God, angels enjoy privileges and powers superior to those of humans, and become involved with humanity in order to protect and guide us, and illuminate our spiritual evolution.

The following chapters explain that while each of us has a guiding or guardian angel, there are many other angels we can call on to help us any time, including circumstances where special abilities or knowledge are required. The angelic presence brings a sense of strength and peace, enables us to benefit from their wisdom and power, and helps us focus on our mission and purpose. Communicating with angels can increase our happiness, and bring us closer to God. Angels cannot violate our free-will – what we do is still up to us – but we should wish for them to be part of our lives.

What do angels look like?

Beings of light, angels are usually invisible to us on earth. However, on occasion they do appear to humans in a range of guises that are acceptable to, or understood by, the people they are contacting (see Chapter 4 for some contemporary examples and experiences). Those who claim to have seen an angel usually describe them as a person, generally male-looking, who foretells key moments of their lives or who assists them with difficult situations. When the task they came to do is accomplished, the angel disappears immediately.

For many centuries, the gender of angels was a matter of some debate. Sacred texts refer to the angels in masculine terms (among other descriptions, the Bible speaks of 'handsome men', 'a man clothed in linen', and men of 'human form'), although in the Old Testament book of Zachariah appear two female angels: 'Then lifted I up mine eyes, and looked, and, behold, there came out two women, and the wind was in their wings; for they had wings like the wings of a stork…' The majority opinion today is that the angels are androgynous beings, that is to say, without sex, genderless. (For convenience sake, this book and the angel cards refer to angels as 'he/him' but equally the references could be to 'she/her' and should be read and interpreted in that light.)

How we imagine angels to look has undoubtedly been heavily influenced by representations – paintings, stained glass, statues and carvings – made over time by different artists in different cultures. In these works, angels are overwhelmingly depicted as young, gentle, attractive men and women with haloes and wings, wearing flowing robes and often carrying symbols of their station and their mission. These details are the artists' imagination as Biblical accounts attest to angels looking and behaving in a wide variety of ways as they bear messages, warn, lead, reassure or help humans.

Being able to float in the air, however, is an aspect of angels frequently repeated in the Bible (most strikingly in the book of Ezekiel, where two types of angel are described, chapters 1 and 10), showing that angels do not obey the law of gravity.

Some Biblical references to angels

Angels make frequent appearances, and play important roles, in the Bible. Below are some key Biblical references to God's messengers.

After he drove the man out, he placed on the east side of the Garden of Eden cherubim and a flaming sword flashing back and forth to guard the way to the tree of life.

Genesis 3:24

The angel of the Lord found Hagar near a spring in the desert; it was the spring that is beside the road to Shur. And he said, 'Hagar, servant of Sarai, where have you come from, and where are you going?'

Genesis 16:7–8

The Lord appeared to Abraham near the great trees of Mamre while he was sitting at the entrance to his tent in the heat of the day. Abraham looked up and saw three men standing nearby. When he saw them, he hurried from the entrance of his tent to meet them and bowed low to the ground.

Genesis 18:1–13

The two angels arrived at Sodom in the evening, and Lot was sitting in the gateway of the city. When he saw them, he got up to meet them and bowed down with his face to the ground.

Genesis 19:1–22

But the angel of the Lord called out to him from heaven, 'Abraham! Abraham!' 'Here I am', he replied.

Genesis 22:11–18

The Lord, the God of heaven, who brought me out of my father's household and my native land and who spoke to me and promised me on oath, saying, 'To your offspring I will give this land'. He will send his angel before you so that you can get a wife for my son from there.

Genesis 24:7

He had a dream in which he saw a stairway resting on the earth, with its top reaching to heaven, and the angels of God were ascending and descending on it.

Genesis 28:12

See, I am sending an angel ahead of you to guard you along the way and to bring you to the place I have prepared.

Exodus 23:20

Exodus 23:23

My angel will go ahead of you and bring you into the land of the Amorites, Hittites, Perizzites, Canaanites, Hivites and Jebusites, and I will wipe them out.

1 Kings 19:5

Then he lay down under the tree and fell asleep. All at once an angel touched him and said, 'Get up and eat'.

Isaiah 6:2–7

Above him were seraphs, each with six wings: With two wings they covered their faces, with two they covered their feet, and with two they were flying. And they were calling to one another: 'Holy, holy, holy is the Lord Almighty; the whole earth is full of his glory.'

Daniel 6:22

My God sent his angel, and he shut the mouths of the lions. They have not hurt me, because I was found innocent in his sight. Nor have I ever done any wrong before you, O king.

Daniel 9:21

While I was still in prayer, Gabriel, the man I had seen in the earlier vision, came to me in swift flight about the time of the evening sacrifice.

Daniel 10:5–7

I looked up and there before me was a man dressed in linen, with a belt of the finest gold around his waist. His body was like chrysolite, his face like lightning, his eyes like flaming torches, his arms and legs like the gleam of burnished bronze, and his voice like the sound of a multitude. I, Daniel, was the only one who saw the vision; the men with me did not see it, but such terror overwhelmed them that they fled and hid themselves.

Zachariah 1:9–19

I asked, 'What are these, my lord?' The angel who was talking with me answered, 'I will show you what they are'. Then the man standing among the myrtle trees explained, 'They are the ones the Lord has sent to go throughout the earth'. And they reported to the angel of the Lord, who was standing among the myrtle trees, 'We have gone throughout the earth and found the whole world at rest and in peace'.

But after he had considered this, an angel of the Lord appeared to him in a dream and said, 'Joseph son of David, do not be afraid to take Mary home as your wife, because what is conceived in her is from the Holy Spirit'.

Matthew 1:20

The Son of Man will send out his angels, and they will weed out of his kingdom everything that causes sin and all who do evil. They will throw them into the fiery furnace, where there will be weeping and gnashing of teeth.

Matthew 13:41–42

See that you do not look down on one of these little ones. For I tell you that their angels in heaven always see the face of my Father in heaven.

Matthew 18:10

Do you think I cannot call on my Father, and he will at once put at my disposal more than twelve legions of angels?

Matthew 26:53

In the sixth month, God sent the angel Gabriel to Nazareth, a town in Galilee, to a virgin pledged to be married to a man named Joseph, a descendant of David. The virgin's name was Mary. The angel went to her and said, 'Greetings, you who are highly favored! The Lord is with you.' Mary was greatly troubled at his words and wondered what kind of greeting this might be. But the angel said to her, 'Do not be afraid, Mary, you have found favour with God. You will be with child and give birth to a son, and you are to give him the name Jesus. He will be great and will be called the Son of the Most High. The Lord God will give him the throne of his father David, and he will reign over the house of Jacob forever; his kingdom will never end.'

Luke 1:26–38

An angel of the Lord appeared to them, and the glory of the Lord shone around them, and they were terrified. But the angel said to them, Do not be afraid. I bring you good news of great joy that will be for all the people. Today in the town of David a

Luke 2:9–14

Saviour has been born to you; he is Christ the Lord. This will be a sign to you: You will find a baby wrapped in cloths and lying in a manger.' Suddenly a great company of the heavenly host appeared with the angel, praising God and saying, 'Glory to God in the highest, and on earth peace to men on whom his favour rests.'

Acts 5:17–21

Then the high priest and all his associates, who were members of the party of the Sadducees, were filled with jealousy. They arrested the apostles and put them in the public jail. But during the night an angel of the Lord opened the doors of the jail and brought them out. 'Go, stand in the temple courts,' he said, 'and tell the people the full message of this new life'.

2 Corinthians 11:13–15

For such men are false apostles, deceitful workmen, masquerading as apostles of Christ. And no wonder, for Satan himself masquerades as an angel of light. It is not surprising, then, if his servants masquerade as servants of righteousness. Their end will be what their actions deserve.

Galatians 4:14

Even though my illness was a trial to you, you did not treat me with contempt or scorn. Instead, you welcomed me as if I were an angel of God, as if I were Christ Jesus himself.

Colossians 1:16

For by him all things were created: things in heaven and on earth, visible and invisible, whether thrones or powers or rulers or authorities; all things were created by him and for him.

Jude 1:6

And the angels who did not keep their positions of authority but abandoned their own home — these he has kept in darkness, bound with everlasting chains for judgement on the great Day.

Revelations 5:11

Then I looked and heard the voice of many angels, numbering thousands upon thousands, and ten thousand times ten thousand. They encircled the throne and the living creatures and the elders.

All the angels were standing around the throne and around the elders and the four living creatures. They fell down on their faces before the throne and worshipped God.

Revelations 7:11

I, John, am the one who heard and saw these things. And when I had heard and seen them, I fell down to worship at the feet of the angel who had been showing them to me. But he said to me, 'Do not do it! I am a fellow servant with you and with your brothers the prophets and of all who keep the words of this book. Worship God!'

Revelations 22:8–9

Angels in the scriptures

Christianity

The Bible tells us that all the angels were created at the same time by God at the beginning of the universe, and are immortal. That they are mentioned so much in the scriptures – around 300 times in the Bible, from Genesis to Revelations – is an indication of their leading role in representing God and acting for Him. It was, for example, an angel who expelled Adam and Eve when they decided to eat that apple in the Garden of Eden, angels who heralded the arrival of the new Messiah, and were present at his birth and resurrection. Ethereal beings, spiritual messengers and intermediaries, angels are still at work today bridging the gap between the material and the divine, between the microcosm (that is, the human) and the macrocosm (the universe).

The Bible speaks of angels as early as the start of Genesis, the first book of the Old Testament, in the verses that describe the beginning of the world when 'God created the heaven and the earth', giving life from nothingness to spiritual beings called angels, in order that they glorify Him. 'In six days Yahve made the heavens and earth, the sea, and all that swam in it, and in Him were created all the things of Heaven and Earth, the visible and the invisible, the thrones, the dominions, the principalities, the powers.' (Thrones, dominions, principalities and powers are all hierarchies of angels, as explained later in this chapter.)

Above all, the Old Testament underlines the special participation of the angels in celebrating the glory due to God as Creator, as in the psalm: 'Praise ye him, all his angels: praise ye him, all his hosts' *(Psalm 148: 2)*. The last verse of Psalm 103, 'Bless the Lord, ye his angels, that excel in strength, that do his commandments, hearkening unto the voice of his word' reveals that angels take part, in their own way, in the government of God over Creation as 'powerful executors of his orders'.

The angels are particularly entrusted to care for and listen to the solicitudes of mankind, on behalf of whom they present requests and orations to God; for example, Psalm 91: 11 proclaims: 'For he shall give his angels charge over thee, to keep thee in all thy ways'. According to the book of Daniel, the function of angels as ambassadors of the living God not only extends to each person but also to whole nations.

The New Testament emphasises the role of angels in relation to the mission of Christ as the Messiah and, above all, in relation to the mystery of the incarnation of the Son of God. It highlights the important part the angels played in the annunciation of the births of John the Baptist and of Christ himself; in the statements made to Mary and Joseph; and in the protection of the newborn Child from Herod's persecution.

Further on, the gospels allude to the presence of angels during Jesus' 40-day fast in the desert and during the speech at Gethsemane *(Luke 22: 43)*. After the resurrection of Christ, it was an angel who told the women who had gone to the tomb of Christ and been surprised to find it empty: 'Be not affrighted: Ye seek Jesus of Nazareth, which was crucified: he is risen; he is not here: behold the place where they laid him. But go your way, tell his disciples.' *(Mark 16: 6–7)*.

Mary Magdalene, who was privileged to see Jesus Himself at the tomb, also saw two angels, while others appeared to the apostles after the disappearance of Christ. They asked, 'Men of Galilee, what are you looking at in the heavens? That Jesus who has been taken from you into heaven will descend from heaven again.'

In his letter addressed to the Ephesians, St Paul says that at the resurrection of Christ, 'He is sat at the right hand of the father…above all principalities, powers and dominions and all that have names, not only in this century, but also in that to come'. *(Ephesians 1: 20–21)* Paul also refers to the angels in his letter to the Colossians: '…For by him were all things created, that are in heaven, and that are in earth, visible and invisible, whether they be thrones, or dominions, or principalities, or powers: all things were created by him, and for him.'

Judaism

As mentioned, the Old Testament is full of angelic encounters, with those described in Genesis, Exodus, Ezekiel, Zachariah and Daniel of particular religious and historic note. The four main archangels, Michael, Gabriel, Raphael and Uriel, are also seen as important, especially Michael in his role as guardian of Israel.

Jews view angels as messengers of God, but in carrying out His will in relation to humans they do not take human form. In addition to the Torah (the first five books of the Old Testament), the Talmud (rabbinical writings), Jewish apocryphal writings and Jewish folklore all have much to say concerning angels, and also demons or dybbuks (malevolent spirits).

Islam

Angels play an important role in Islam. The Koran repeatedly refers to angels as celestial beings, an army of God who live in a paradise or divine world. Muslims believe that each believer has two guardian angels who record all that they do in their lifetime.

Islam, however, does not view angels as having a physical form, although it is recognised that they can appear in various guises in dreams and visions. Of the numerous angels mentioned in the Koran, five are of special significance and power:

- Gibrael or Gabriel, who revealed the Koran to Muhammed.

- Israfil, who is entrusted with calling, with his trumpet, the souls in order to consecrate them in the Final Judgement.

- Isra'il, bringer of the message of death.

- Mikal or Michael, messenger and intermediary between the divinity and mankind.

- Iblis (or Shaytan – Satan or the devil), the perverse angel who rebelled against God and who tricked Adam and Eve in the garden of Eden. For this he is condemned to Hell. Satan is a jinn, an angel who is now entrusted with ruling Hell until the day of the Final Judgement. At the end of time, it is possible that the devil will have paid for his sins and can return to the side of God, in Heaven. In the meantime his mission is to tempt and confuse humans in order to keep them apart from God. One of his goals is to convince people of the divinity of Muhammed, despite it having been made clear that there is no God but Allah and Muhammed is his messenger.

Angelic classifications

Despite their closeness to God, not all angels are the same, nor do they have the same tasks or responsibilities. Over the centuries, many theologians and scholars have studied the various hierarchies or orders to which angels appear to belong, and what each stands for. According to this tradition, the 'Nine Choirs of Angels' or angelic orders are as listed below. (Seraphim and cherubim are mentioned only in the

Old Testament, while the New Testament mentions the seven others.)

- seraphim
- cherubim
- thrones
- dominions (order only what is needed to be done)
- virtues (those who work miracles)
- powers (those who counteract adverse powers)
- principalities (those who preside over good spirits)
- archangels (the messengers of higher things)
- guardian angels (the messengers of things of lesser importance).

The first triad or hierarchy: this consists of cherubim, seraphim, and thrones. These angels dedicate themselves exclusively to glorifying, loving and praising God in His presence.

The second triad or hierarchy: this consists of dominions, virtues and powers. Governing space and the stars, they are responsible for the whole universe.

The third triad or hierarchy: this consists of principalities, archangels and angels. These are the angels who intervene on our behalf, each one with a mission given by God Himself. They are entrusted with protecting nations, cities and churches. The vision of the prophet Daniel confirms this mission *(Daniel 7: 8)*, as does the passage from Apocalypse *(1: 20)* when it refers to the angels of the seven churches.

(The 72 angel cards which accompany this book feature a coloured frame around each picture of an angel. The frame denotes the hierarchy to which the angel belongs. Blue frames indicate seraphim, purple frames cherubim, red frames thrones, turquoise frames powers, red frames dominions, light green frames principalities, purple frames archangels, green frames virtues, and orange frames guardian angels.)

The first hierarchy
Seraphim

Seraphim are only mentioned in the scriptures in the vision of Isaiah (where they are spoken of as having six wings); the word itself can be interpreted as 'serpent', 'burn', 'ardent', or even 'wheels of fire'. Angels of love, of light and of fire, seraphim are considered to be the highest order of the celestial hierarchy and the most beautiful beings in Heaven. The beings closest to God, they surround His throne and constantly praise Him, singing: 'Holy, holy, holy is the Lord of hosts…' They are said to generate the heat of love around themselves, and to give out a light that never wanes and drives out darkness.

In order to attract seraphim into your life, it is useful to read them poetry or fairytales, as they have a childlike innocence.

Cherubim

The name *cherub* signifies 'fullness of knowledge, or overflowing with wisdom, whose extreme intelligence permits them to know God as no human could'. Cherubim are mentioned in the first book of the Bible, which tells of the sin of Adam and Eve: 'So he drove out the man; and he placed at the east of the garden of Eden Cherubims, and a flaming sword which turned every way, to keep the way of the tree of life' *(Genesis 3: 24)*.

Wise beings or celestial masters, cherubim guard
the throne of God, light and the stars, and the gates
of Eden. Their role is also that of record keepers and
delegators. They have often been depicted historically as
having four faces and four or more wings, although the
popular conception of them is often as small, plump,
winged infants.

Cherubim are attracted by toys, sweets, and brightly
coloured objects.

Thrones

The principal mission of thrones is the same as the
seraphim and cherubim; that is, to contemplate and
adore God. The personal advisors of God, responsible
for giving the highest level of goodness and pureness
to Heaven, the thrones control the universal order, so
that everything in time and space occurs at the right
moment. Impassive, serene and balanced beings,
thrones are just, judicious, and free of all baseness or
iniquity.

Thrones look different from other celestial beings
and have been described as burning wheels, the rims
of which are covered with hundreds of eyes. These are
said to be the wheels that drive the chariot of God.

**The second
hierarchy**

Dominions

The dominions create physical and dynamic laws
in order to synchronise the world. These beings
are melancholic and deeply versed in the mysteries
of creation, sensitive to mystic atmospheres, and
illuminated by white candles, perfumed with incense
and myrrh. They are usually depicted wearing a crown

and bearing a sceptre; sometimes they appear dressed as soldiers and carrying a sword in their hand.

Virtues

The virtues materialise the divine desires and give the appropriate form, colour and scent to each thing. Carriers of grace and courage, their principal task is to work miracles on the earth, and bestow encouragement and blessings. It is traditionally believed that the angels presiding over the Ascension of Jesus were virtues, a fact that seems to be confirmed by the smell of incense reported to surround the tomb of Christ.

Powers

It is said that this order of angels is shaped like brightly coloured, hazy fumes and that they govern the stars and the elements of nature. The mission of the powers is to protect the world in general, and oversee the distribution of power among mankind. They bestow energy on all living beings, including what are known as auras.

The third hierarchy

Principalities

The principal mission of principalities is to care for humanity, especially in times of hardship, and to concern themselves with the issues and events relating to countries and their rulers.

In some paintings principalities appear dressed as warriors or as deacons, and they carry a lily. As their habitual dwelling is in the vegetable and mineral kingdoms, it is recommended that they be invoked in a place of abundant vegetation.

Archangels

The archangels are the officials of Heaven, the princes of God's army. They carry out tasks which relate to the affairs of mankind. They are considered saints. There are four main ones: Michael, who has supreme authority, and his lieutenants Gabriel, Raphael, and Uriel, the final two letters of all these names signifying 'of God'.

Archangel Michael (He who is as God):
Archangel Michael, who ranks as 'chief of the celestial hosts', appears in both the Old and the New Testaments and the Koran. In the book of Daniel, this angel gives strength to the prophet in difficult times of invasions and war. Michael is also described as an archangel by Judas, and spoken of as being in a battle, implying that he is a military leader.

Michael's image represents justice, important changes, understanding of things, and our own alignment with the universe. He encourages us to fight for just and noble causes; he gives us the courage and strength to stand up for what is right, especially when persecuted.

Michael is the best protector of human beings against disruptive elements, and for this reason it is not uncommon to see in some countries his representational sphinx on doorways and openings. He is of such importance that he has churches exclusively dedicated to him, and prayers in both churches and synagogues that specifically ask for his help.

The protector of towns and cities, Michael is represented with armour and a sword (although he can be found carrying a lance, representing the Power of God, with which he destroys Satan). The sword, double edged, represents the word of God, which confuses lies and dispels illusions. If your problem is a very powerful adversary, invoke the help of Michael.

The following characteristics are associated with St Michael the archangel:

- Colour: blue, the colour of emotion.
- Season: winter.
- Element: fire.
- Hours: the night, specifically midnight.

Archangel Raphael (God cures): Known as 'the healer'. St Raphael is frequently depicted adorned with botanical symbols. He can hand us the gift of healing, help us to achieve a sense of wholeness in mind and body, and guide us to discover a cure in nature. He also assists when we wish to heal our fellow beings.

St Raphael is often depicted as dressed in a robe tied with a belt, carrying a staff in the shape of a sceptre in his right hand, symbolising both power and the support he gives to those who ask for his assistance. He is a consoler in present difficulties and a help with afflictions and all types of suffering, even those which seem unbearable. St Raphael represents physical force, personal brilliance and success. He inspires loyalty and nobleness, as well as providing the gift of leadership. He is the patron of all who repent.

The following characteristics are associated with St Raphael the archangel:

- Colour: red.
- Season: autumn.
- Element: earth.
- Hours: nightfall, from 6 pm.

Archangel Gabriel (Prince of God or Fortress of God): A special messenger of the Holy Ghost, it was Gabriel who told the prophet Daniel of the coming of Christ, and it is for this reason that he enjoys privileges that place him alongside the archangel Michael.

Mentioned four times in the Bible, St Gabriel is considered as being the mediator between Heaven and the humans, the announcer of messages (among them the births of special children, one of whom was Jesus), and the divulger of divine words. The Bible stories tell of how Gabriel stayed the hand of Abraham when he was about to kill his son Isaac by divine order; made water spring in the desert so that Ishmael could drink; and, most importantly, told Joseph to flee when Herod was intent on killing male babies.

St Gabriel is frequently depicted with a lily – a symbol of purity – in paintings of the annunciation of Mary. His tasks are to give to mankind messages of love, brotherhood and liberty, and to help us to express our truth openly and honestly, to honour our individuality, and to follow our intuition and our inner voice. Those who suffer greatly, for physical and other reasons, should invoke Gabriel to come to their aid.

The following characteristics are associated with St Gabriel the archangel:

- Colour: green.
- Season: spring.
- Element: water.
- Hours: midday.

Archangel Uriel (Light of God, Fire of God):
Of the four major archangels, Uriel is the least known,
or the one who is least written about. He is often
depicted with one bare foot and the other with a shoe,
and he carries an olive bough, signifying peace. He is
also often shown with a thick book of wisdom in his
left hand.

St Uriel is not mentioned in the traditional Bible but
in some of the holy books of the Jews of ancient times
and other writings. Legend has it that this angel stood
at the gate of the lost paradise of Eden, with a flaming
sword, to prevent Adam and Eve from returning.

The angel of repentance, Uriel is considered the
guardian of the West, of emotions and of the heart.
He reminds humanity that it should love God, and shows
us the way of the heart and the fire of pure love. He can
help us to recognise the light that is inside each person, to
find what we need to know to help and protect ourselves
and others, and to interpret our inner voice.

The following characteristics are associated with the
archangel Uriel:

- Colour: yellow.
- Season: summer.
- Element: air.
- Hours: dawn.

Angels

The angels are the most abundant of celestial beings
in terms of numbers. The closest of the heavenly
hierarchy to mankind and the world, the ones who
show themselves to us, they are divided into two groups:
the builders and the guardians. The former control

everything concerning the spirit, the ether, and the four basic elements of life, and the latter group occupy themselves with human beings and nature. The angels can be seen in different forms and colours.

What do angels do?

One of the main things angels do is to give guidance and convey messages about all kinds of things. If you wish to consult an angel about a particular matter, an appropriate one is something related to the present time and the action that you should take. You can ask, for example, about a personal or social relationship, your work or studies, about buying or selling a business, moving house, making an investment, or bringing about some other kind of change in your life. It is crucial to ask your question in a way that it can be clearly understood by the angel; for example, 'The problem is my relationship with…' You should not expect the angel to make a decision for you, because they are perfect souls and will never interfere with your thoughts. However, you can say, 'I am thinking of doing…', 'Would it be right to…?' If you do not have a specific question in mind, you can say, 'What do I need in order to make my life more pleasant and satisfying?' or 'What do I need to work on at this moment?'

Once you feel your angel is present, ask the question out loud or in your thoughts and wait for the angel to reply, then or later. Remember to show your positive side, or you will spoil the atmosphere. Although you would probably like your angel to reply with a clear 'yes' or 'no', he may be much more subtle than that. Ask a question and wait for the angel to reply in his own way, now or later.

However it comes, the response will always be instructive and apt. If you receive information that seems wrong, illogical or false, it is possible that this is due to a negative way of asking. You should stop communication immediately and ask God for His protection and blessing. Then reframe the question in a clearer or more positive way.

Making contact with angels

Chapter 2 sets out some specific means, as well as prayers and invocations, for bringing angels into your life, and Chapter 3 tells how to use the 72 angel cards that accompany this book to connect with particular angels. The method that works for you is the right way. The truth that will transform your life and feed your spirit comes from within yourself. Your angel will give you the best information from the highest divine source; you must then assume responsibility for what you hear and try to carry out the advice you are given.

Angels may come in dreams or in visions, or we can call on them, or just be open and ready for contact. Normally, a prayer or invocation is used to contact angels and ask them for help or for consolation. But angels can appear, or angelic help can occur, without someone asking or even believing.

Angels deliver their messages through a variety of channels and we should be attentive to the subtle ways in which this can happen. Sometimes they do so clearly and personally; often it is simply through a phrase in a book, a message that suddenly seems to speak to us, or something that appears before us for apparently no reason. We must be open to these signs and not consider anything a coincidence.

In an angelic presence, some people feel shivers or a premonition, others feel happy or inspired. Sometimes a pleasant fragrance can be detected or there is music. Any one of these signs can show that our guardian angel is close; all that we have to do is ask a question and wait for a reply.

Your spiritual growth is the best contribution that you can make to yourself. As you work on this growth, what you want and need in your life will become clearer. Your guardian angel can help you to achieve your purpose. As you refine your thoughts, actions and intentions through this process, you will achieve a higher spiritual conscience and friendship with the angelic kingdom. Ask and you shall be given.

Angelic communication

As we have seen, angels communicate with humans in many ways – speaking the language of the person they are interacting with, or transmitting their message through a voice in the head, as a whisper, a thought. They can also use visual means, or a scent to indicate their presence. When communication takes place with a higher being, the means may be subtle but the message is fluent and clear, without confusion, and appropriate to the ability and intellectual level of the person.

When an angel speaks, the centre of energy at the crown of the head, the crown chakra related to the pituitary gland, is activated. When this centre is activated the sound is spectacularly clear; no sound reproduction system on earth can reproduce such clarity and make such an impression on our memory. There is no need to make any effort to remember what an angel says because, if such communication is established, the impression is enormous and it is impossible to forget a single word.

To encourage angels to communicate with you, first cultivate a peaceful frame of mind and loving attitude to yourself and others. Empty your heart of negativity, let your best feelings flow, and ask the angels for what you need – assistance, guidance or protection or anything that is positive. Do not be disheartened if at first you don't achieve contact. Sometimes the angels approach slowly, placing weak signals in your path so that you become aware of them, until the moment arrives when the messages are unmistakeable. You should use the enrichment you receive to help others.

It is recommended that you do not talk about your communication with angels to those who do not believe in them, as this is a waste of energy, will disconcert you, and in time may cause you to doubt what you have experienced. Keep your faith strong and feed your spiritual communication. Your conviction in what you see, hear and feel is your best weapon against scepticism and disbelief.

The messages from the angels can be used for oneself or for other people. When others are present, it is very important that all the participants desire, and are open to, a positive contact with the angels.

Guardian angels

Although the majority of people are not conscious of the presence of this protecting being at their side, we all have a personal guardian angel, assigned at our birth. Their role is to care for us, protect us and advise us throughout our life. Our guardian angel also acts as a 'voice of conscience', trying to help and guide us on our path of learning; consoling us in moments of sadness or difficulty; and often granting us our wishes when we make some sort of direct request (given that it is for good and does not interfere in the free-will of others).

Our guardian angel is our best and closest friend, at our side throughout our whole life. He is always awake, constantly ready to give us his help at times of temptation or difficulty. It is a shame if, because of forgetfulness, half-heartedness or ignorance, we do not let ourselves enjoy the presence of this faithful companion, nor ask for his assistance as often as we need it. Although we must not worship angels, we owe our guardian angel veneration as one who is always in the presence of God, contemplating Him face to face at the same time as being next to us. Experiences of contact with guardian angels are as varied as the people that have them but, in general, great emotion is felt at the first contact, like finding an old friend.

One of the things our guardian angel does is to enable us to be a channel of his energy in order to transmit it to assist other people. Through this energy we can modify the emotional state of another (which can affect their physical state, including ailments, as many illnesses are emotional in origin) as these personal angels work principally with the emotional field. The person receiving this transmission of energy will have a closer relation with their own guardian angel for a period, even if they are unaware of this. This contact attracts all sorts of positive events to the person.

Our guardian angels have names in the same way that people do. The name of our angel is related to ourselves and has something to do with our vibration, our level of consciousness, and our potential. It is not necessary to know the name of our angel, but where we do, using it allows us to connect more easily and more directly with his energy, accelerating our spiritual growth (see Chapter 2 for more on this subject).

The nature of a guardian angel confers many powers. However, despite being of the greatest perfection when compared to humans, an angel:

- does not know the secrets of God
- does not know the destiny of mankind
- knows our actions better than our thoughts
- cannot see the future, not even his own, although he can give us warnings.

Ways our guardian angels can help us

Guardian angels can help us in many ways:

1. Guide and protect us (and all people, even if they do not believe).
2. Assist with both everyday and more complex life matters.
3. Transmit energy.
4. Help us to connect with other angels and to receive angelic messages through other people or situations.
5. Help us to develop luck or take advantage of chance or opportunity.
6. Help us relate to our peers or in connection with a particular task, such as arriving on time at a certain place.
7. Help us find work.
8. Make our lives easier.
9. Enable us to identify the things that we have to modify or change.
10. Help us to find the inner answer.
11. Act as the voice of our conscience.
12. Warn us of something through our intuition. It is up to us to listen to that interior voice, as the angels warn but do not oblige.

Listening to our guardian angel

Look for your angel in your heart and tell him you wish to talk. Can you see the image of your angel yet? Can you sense his presence? Connect with him and have the benefit of him in your life. Stretch your imagination and don't underestimate what you are feeling. If this doesn't work for you now, try again another time, directing a prayer to ask for His protection and that He guide you in your communication with the angel.

Our guardian angels are always with us, observers of our difficulties and attentive helpers that alleviate our pain, teachers, masters and loving companions. But too often we ignore their existence, and very often we do quite the opposite to what they advise us. But although the work of our angel is not always recognised and appreciated, their love remains constant and their patience is infinite. While only God knows exactly what lies in our hearts, angels can, however, know a great deal about us in a similar way to which other people pick up information. We can also suppose that the angels have done us many favours without us even knowing. Tradition says that angels will do us more favours if we trust in them.

A good relationship with the angels requires spiritual openness and a willingness to accept others and to understand ourselves better. Very little is needed to change our habits to embrace our guardian angel. A thought in the morning, a smile or a small prayer can be sufficient to change our day and to make us feel more serene, confident, and more conscious that we are not, and have never been, alone.

To lead us on the path to obedience and love, the angel sets up a silent communication with our soul. He inspires us with thoughts that help us to avoid falling into bad ways or making mistakes. He 'suggests' taking one path instead of another, discouraging us from taking grave risks. He can make the things that we should do blossom in our minds, or push away things that we should not do. He incites us to reflect on and fight against our weaknesses, to work towards our ideals, and to continually feed our inner self so that it does not starve.

To these ends, the guardian angel whispers his advice to our soul and not to our ears. However, given that we possess free-will, he cannot intervene against our wishes. We are free to accept or reject his appeals, following the path that he indicates or, persevering in our error, not taking advantage of his help. Sometimes the presence of this heavenly guide is not enough for us to avoid accidents and painful situations – although these would be more numerous if we did not count on his help – but he helps us through the situations we have to deal with.

The angel watches over our soul, but he can also help us in our day-to-day problems and protect our material interests when these are important for our spiritual progress. Your angel will always remain by your side, wishing to intervene on your behalf and to accede to your requests. However, his actions will always be devalued if he never truly achieves contact with you, the person to whom he has been entrusted. On the other hand, those who knowingly direct themselves to their guardian angel, opening their heart to his silent words, asking him questions in times of need, and seeking contact with him, can count on the valuable help of this loyal friend. Listening to our angel means letting him have a silent space so that he can help us to clear our minds of the thoughts that keep us tied to a relentless reality, and in this way, establish contact with a higher state of being.

Some questions about angels

We have been led to believe that happiness is obtained through the accumulation of wealth, but this is not so. Angels are here to help us find happiness and the way to God, and will never be able to tell us the numbers that will win the lottery. What they can do is bestow the wisdom necessary in order that we make enough money to live with dignity.

Our true purpose in life is to reach Heaven and to help our fellow man; this is when we truly have all the riches of the world. If we observe those who spend their lives helping others, we will see that they reap rich rewards.

Can the angels help to make people rich?

No. Men and women are different from angels and the Bible does not say that people can become angels after death. Some angels, however, appear on earth in human form in order not to frighten people when carrying out a particular task.

Do people become angels when they die?

The angels are nobody's judge, nor do they pass sentence, as this is the work of God. Furthermore, if we ask them to do harm to someone, it is possible that the angelic forces will turn against us because we are breaking one of the Ten Commandments.

Can an angel punish someone who is doing us harm?

Does carrying a picture, or a symbol, of an angel with us give protection?

No. This is just as mistaken as thinking that praying intensely will get us to Heaven. Pictures or talismans of angels are symbols of faith, but we have to live our own lives, working to improve different aspects and avoiding hurting those around us.

If we are good, will angels help us more?

We should not make judgements about our own virtues as it is easy to deceive ourselves. The angels do not reward or punish, their aim is to carry messages to and protect humans.

Are there angels with particular strengths?

Yes, as can be seen from the descriptions of the angel cards. It is recommended that you invoke these and other angels personally, calling them by their names, focusing on the abilities for which they are best known.

What is the difference between angels and spirits?

Like angels, spirits deliver their messages quickly, can be of a pale, ethereal appearance, and are capable of moving without touching the ground or making any noise. The difference lies in their origin: angels come from and live in Heaven; spirits are worldly beings that previously occupied an earthly body and now wander, waiting for their new destiny.

Evil angels

As we have seen, the major religions recognise the existence of angels or benign and loving spirits whose role is to worship God and help mankind lead good lives. They also recognise the existence of the devil, also referred to as Satan. Christianity in particular places great importance on him and the other fallen angels, and their evil intent of leading humans astray and away from God.

The word Satan – which comes from the Hebrew *satan* meaning 'adversary' or 'resister' – was initially used in the Old Testament to denote the forces of evil, although later on the term 'devil' was more commonly used. Today in speech we tend to use the names interchangeably. Enemy of God, father of lies, wicked, and prince of darkness are other terms applied to the devil, who, we are told, can assume human or animal form in order to tempt mankind and lead us into wrongdoing.

This supreme spirit of evil and of the negative aspects of mankind was not always so. The Bible tells us that the devil is a fallen angel, Lucifer, God's brightest and best, who (in the guise of a serpent) exercised free-will and chose to tempt Adam and Eve to eat fruit forbidden to them by God in the Garden of Eden. For this sin of pride, the devil was cast out of Heaven, and has since acted as a tempter, an impostor and a liar, to cause human beings to disobey God.

Dealing with the devil

In Jewish literature, Satan resides in the lower atmosphere, alongside other demonic and negative powers. In Islam, the devil is known as *shaitan*, and in Hinduism as *asuras*. Although less common, there are also female devils. Buddhist texts mention them as *mara* and they represent evil in the purest sense.

We need to be constantly aware of the devil's presence and prepare ourselves to resist his influence and that of the demons, or fallen angels, associated with him. His powers are immense, and over time his aim of trying to sabotage the work of God has not changed. Despite the undoubted strength of diabolical temptation, however, Satan's malice cannot go beyond God's wishes; his power is great, but controlled. God is faithful, and will not permit you to be tempted beyond your strength (*1 Corinthians 10: 13*). In short, it is best to be in the middle: neither forget the existence of the devil nor the effectiveness of his evil intent, but do not lose faith in God.

The devil has several ways of deceiving us (below are some of his strategies) and drawing us into his web. He cannot oblige us to sin, but he can trick, confuse and pressure us, making us believe that the consequences of our bad actions will not come back on us. His greatest trick is to make us think that he does not exist.

Tempting. Temptation is the devil's way of persuading humans to sin and disobey God, and it leads us to condemning ourselves. It is his most common means of tempting us to do wrong, and his most subtle, as it can catch us off guard.

Besieging. The devil does not leave us alone; in fact he besieges and confuses us. He also places around us things and people who lead us to doing wrong as a way of making ourselves happy.

Obsession. Through this means the devil stops us from analysing our own existence; he clouds our reasoning and incites us to renounce what we believe. He makes us believe that Hell is one of God's creations and that He is therefore a wicked being.

Demons

Demons are fallen angels. The word comes from the Greek *daimones*, which means ethereal beings; these could be good, evil or neutral.

Great quantities of angels, who were also convinced that they could be happy without God, rebelled against God and were cast out of Heaven. Soon after, remorseful for what they had lost, and in despair at not being able to return (the punishment was eternal), the fallen angels sought a means of taking revenge. This took the form of acting against mankind, the highest creation of God; their vengeance towards humans meant they were no longer alone in their place of suffering and punishment.

We need to be wary of evil angels. As our earthly plane is closer to lower realms than higher ones it attracts bad spirits, making it easy to become entangled. Demons delight in corrupting us, encouraging us to become greedy and to disregard spiritual values. Selfish motivation and negative attitudes make us vulnerable to attracting them – and they can be attractive. We need to develop discernment and learn to judge the difference between good and bad – and choose good.

Good angels act as tutors, teaching us by example and inspiration rather than intervening in our learning. Evil angels will manipulate our spiritual destiny, exploit our physical bodies and enslave our souls.

The following is more information on Satan and some of the other fallen angels.

Lucifer

Lucifer, whose name is also translated as 'Drawer of Light' or 'Carrier of Light', is the emperor of hell who, before the exile from heaven, was the most beautiful and perfect of all the angels. Tradition says that Lucifer was one of the seven great archangels of our solar system, being in charge of the planet Venus. It seems that God asked for a volunteer from among his principal angels to go to earth in order to strengthen the spiritual determination of mankind by giving constant temptations. Lucifer offered himself for the task. Unhappily, and in spite of his loving intentions, with the passing of the centuries – especially since the exile from Paradise – he has become connected with the devil, instead of being viewed as an aspect of God that helps us to grow. 'The devil made me do it' continues to be a tempting excuse to justify our behaviour, passing on the guilt of our own actions and painting Lucifer as the source of all that we consider 'evil' in the world.

One of Lucifer's celestial tasks is to teach us about the necessary dark side of life, the shadow that reveals the light by contrast.

Belcebu (or Beelzebub)

The prince of the satanic empire, he is second in the infernal hierarchy, just after Satan. From the Greek Beelzebul, he is the 'Regent of the Demons', also known as the 'Lord of Chaos', 'Lord of the Flies' (in some cultures it was believed that flies carried the souls of the impious to Hell), 'Baal-zebud' or 'Ekron'.

Leviathan

The great admiral of hell, he tempts ordinary humans with honour and fame. For many he is also the demon of the oceans, and as such responsible for the majority of shipwrecks.

Lilith

A female demon, Lilith is thought to have been the first wife of Adam. Wishing to dominate him instead of being his companion, she lost her place as first woman, although it is also believed that she was the mother of Cain. When God created Eve, Lilith was filled with envy and became the enemy of Eve and her children. In this way she joined the ranks of the demons, uniting with them in order to do evil, especially to women.

Mephistopheles

Mephistopheles (which means 'the one who hates the light') is a destroying demon who pronounces the executions in Hell.

Peter

He often appears as an imp who seems to be six or seven years old, with blue eyes and blond hair. He used to have a sweet nature and often laughed and smiled. But when he became evil, he began to inflict terrible pain on his victims. He has a great capacity for lying and tricking people, pretending to be a devout believer. The true form of Peter is humanoid, small, red skinned, winged, and with short horns and a tail.

Connecting with Angels

As already discussed, there are various paths you can follow in order to make contact, and communicate, with angels. You may wish to use the set of 72 angel cards associated with this book in the ways outlined in this and the next chapter, devise your own ways of using the cards, or follow or adapt some of the many other suggestions in this chapter. These last include a range of rituals, procedures, prayers and invocations. Choose whatever feels appropriate for you.

Angelic attitudes

The angels are at our service, waiting for us to invite or allow them to intervene. The following attitudes can encourage them to do so:

1. As angels live in a state of grace, in constant contact with God, the basic emotional state of the angelic realm is one of happiness. If we keep happy and see the positive side of the things that happen to us, this will attract the angels.

2. The techniques and rituals used to make direct contact with the angelic realm are within reach of us all. Although angels can appear to unbelievers, contact will be facilitated if you believe that angels exist and interact with humans for their benefit. Accept that powers reside in the energetic fields of which human beings are composed, and that we may understand little about these powers as yet – except that they can be called on.

3. Entering into direct contact with the energy of the angels changes our vision of the world, as we

become conscious of a divine plan. Always trust
that we are under the protection of God, as this
confidence and faith allow us to make contact. Fear
and external negativity must be pushed aside.

4. In the dimension of the angels, everything is simple
   and perfect; good and evil do not exist, there is no
   space and time. Even though it may feel like we
   have spent hours making contact with the angels, it
   is possible that only a few minutes or seconds have
   passed.

5. On our path of learning in this dimension, we
   can count on all the help we need. As is written in
   Matthew 7: 7, 'Ask, and it shall be given you; seek,
   and ye shall find; knock, and it shall be opened unto
   you'. But the decision to access this help is yours
   alone, because human beings have free-will.

How to relate to angels

In the right frame of mind, isolate yourself from
distractions and remain quietly in your chosen place.
Commune with the angels simply by talking to them
about your problems the same as you would with your
best friend. Then be silent and listen, waiting for the
thoughts that they place in your mind. (Further on in
this chapter, particular rituals are outlined that you can
follow if you wish.)

Make a space in your life for angels

If you want the angels to feel comfortable with you,
then you must make your world, thoughts, feelings
and surroundings more like their own. Angels feel

comfortable with thoughts of peace and love rather than thoughts of irritation and aggressiveness. And rather than always asking for something, it is better to meditate on your behaviour and resolve to treat others the way you would wish to be treated.

Say prayers out loud

Angels have replied to many silent prayers and intense, heartfelt desires. But if you wish to speak out loud, do so, because your voice has power. Addressing God and the angels can take various spoken forms: songs and hymns, structured and unstructured prayers. These can be combined with *fiats* (permission or orders) and decrees. The *fiats* are short, powerful affirmations. The decrees allow God to work together with mankind to make constructive changes. Make your decrees and *fiats* in a strong, clear voice.

Use the name of God

God is inside you and by using His energy when you address yourself to the angels they will be able to respond to you with all the power of the universe.

The Fire of God is what makes you His son or daughter. This Divine Spark is the power to create in the name of God and to make requests of the angels. Each time you say, 'I am...', you are in reality saying, 'God in me is...' In this way, you bring to yourself that which you ask for.

Offer your prayers and decrees every day

It is up to you how often you connect with the angels through prayer and other means, but it is best is to commune with them every day. By doing so, you not only help yourself but also many people who you do not even know. The angels look for people who habitually invoke the light of God in order to join with them and help cure the planet. When they find these people, they send light from themselves to help other men and women who are in danger or suffering. Your prayers can make great changes without you being aware of them.

The prayers and decrees are more effective when they are repeated because more light is given to God and the angels each time that you say them. The angels use this energy as if it were a seed, adding more light energy when they respond to your request.

Repeat the decrees and prayers

Even after establishing a relationship with the angels, you must still remember to ask for help if you need it. The angels respect your free-will and will only rarely intercede without you having asked them to do so. They normally wait politely until they are called.

Ask for help

The angels respond to calls with precision and are proud of doing so. The more specific the petition, the more specific the reply. When you live in harmony with the Universal Source and dedicate your energy to helping others, the angelic hosts will help you in even the smallest detail of your life.

If the problem you wish to resolve is very great, or involves others, consider getting together various members of the family or a group of affected people in order to jointly ask for help. Where two or more people are in conflict, the best solution is for them to pray together for the same wish that they be reunited.

Send your prayers in the right direction

If you need protection, call on the angels of protection. If you want to mend a relationship, call on the angels of love. The angels have their different jobs and use different energies of different frequencies in order to carry out their tasks. Moreover, you can reach a more intimate level of contact with them when you call those that are specialised in your area of need.

Visualise what you wish to happen

You can increase the power of your prayer by keeping an intense image in your mind of that which you wish to happen. Furthermore, you can visualise a bright light around the problem or situation. It can also be a help to concentrate on a relevant photograph as you make your petition.

Some specific visualisations you could use for connecting with angels and archangels are given later in this chapter.

Expect surprises

The angels listen to all prayers but, in order for the petitions to be granted, they should follow three conditions: they must not interfere with God's plan for your soul, or with your 'karma'; they cannot be damaging to yourself or other people; the moment must be appropriate.

A prayer to an angel is always fruitful, you simply have to know where to look. When you pray, eat or prepare to sleep or wake up, give special thanks to the angels.

Angelic rituals

The following will give you some ideas for creating a welcoming and uplifting space where you can work on contacting your angel.

Invoking the protection of the angels through a ritual can bring good heath, peace, harmony, prosperity and personal success. A ritual is an established procedure to make sure that a ceremony is carried out properly. A basic element in invoking protection and help is a hand-drawn ritualised sketch of an angel. If you know who you are calling on, include the name of the angel and your own name.

To carry out your ritual, choose a quiet place that is suitable for meditation and where you can play and enjoy special music (see page 52). Make sure you will not be interrupted by people, doorbells or phones.

It is helpful to sit in the lotus position, with your palms facing upwards, and breathe slowly and deeply in and out. (Alternatively you may wish to assume the position described on page 52.) Allow any tension in the body to melt away, and thoughts or problems that come into your mind to drift off.

Ambience

The angels are delicate creatures, sensitive to aromas, and so the room you use for your ritual should be cleaned and ventilated before starting. It is recommended that you then burn some incense or place a vase of fresh flowers in the room, or add some lemon or orange peel to give a pleasant smell. You could also arrange some other offerings, which should be beautiful: a reproduction of a painting of angels, a statue, a ceramic angel, etc.

Lighting

The angels are not very comfortable in bright places, with their contrasts of light and shadow. Soft lighting or semidarkness is appropriate; after all, it is they who will bring the light. Lighting some white candles will give you ideal illumination.

Appropriate music

The symphonies of Brahms and Handel, romances for violin and orchestra by Beethoven, *Eine Kleine Nachtmusik* by Mozart, Vivaldi's *Four Seasons*, Gregorian chanting, children's music (in soft tones) and New Age music (Enya, Vangelis, Ian Anderson) are all particularly useful for attracting protecting angels. Play them as often as you can.

Posture

If you prefer to sit, take off your shoes and loosen any tight clothing. Sit in a chair with your feet resting on the floor, parallel and about twenty centimetres apart. Rest your hands on your knees with your palms facing upwards, keeping the back straight.

Breathing

Concentrate on your breathing, paying attention to the flow of the air inside your body with each inhalation and exhalation. This will help you empty your mind.

Start by focusing and connecting your energy with the earth. Breathe deeply through your nose and, at the same time, imagine that a tree of white light is descending from above to your head. While you exhale through your mouth, continue to imagine the tree of light descending through your body and reaching the earth.

Offer a prayer, proclamation or invocation such as those in this chapter, or use one of your own. If you wish, you can write your proclamation or invocation down, as well as saying it aloud, and place it in your special place.

A means of connecting

Remember, the angels are messengers, divine emissaries of God, and therefore your communication with them reaches God directly. It doesn't matter which name you use to address Him. God, Goddess, Mother, Power, Father, Almighty, Great Spirit, Creator, Allah, Jesus, Buddha or Krishna: all are the very same entity. Your intention is what counts.

Visualising angels

As part of the above ritual or separately from it, you can use visualisations to connect with angels. The following are two suggested visualisations, or you can devise your own:

Visualisation 1

1. Imagine that you are beneath a dark blue sky on a quiet night. Look up to find the stars and count them. Even though there are many of them and each one gleams with its own light, try to observe all those luminous points that dance and move in the sky. If you look closely, you will notice that there is one star that vibrates with particular brightness. Isolate that star and observe it shine in the sky; it seems to shine only for you.

2. While you are observing it, the star begins to move slowly, perhaps crossing the sky, and to descend.

The star grows larger, becoming closer and brighter, seeming to illuminate the whole sky. Pay close attention to the centre of the star and see that a figure begins to form, this image moving closer and closer.

3. The light gives a feeling of peace and wellbeing. Allow your heart to vibrate in the direction of the light and synchronise with it.

4. You are about to find your angel. Let him approach with trust, and enjoy the feeling of waiting and the emotion that it brings.

5. Be attentive to each sensation, each nuance, each colour.

6. Enjoy the feeling of peace and tranquillity, and at the same time, the joy that grows inside you, the security of being protected and feeling safe.

7. Concentrate on the contact established between your heart and the vibration of the angel's light. It is now the moment to send your message to the angel. First, give him thanks for having answered your call, and then make your petition.

8. You can ask for help, protection and advice about a specific problem or just enjoy this extraordinary contact, being happy to have experienced it.

9. Finally, give thanks, promise love, and say goodbye, asking for the chance to have other encounters.

10. The light will move away and become a star again.

11. Keep the sensation of this marvellous contact within yourself as well as the sure knowledge that the angel will never abandon you.

Choose an appropriate time and place so that you **Visualisation 2**
will not be interrupted. Disconnect the telephone, turn
off the mobile and, if possible, the doorbell. Sit in a
comfortable chair and close your eyes.

Imagine that you are walking along a path that runs
through a gently sloping valley.

You feel the path and the living earth beneath your
feet. The air is calm and fresh, with a slight breeze
which caresses your face. There is a soft scent of flowers
in the air.

In the valley is a small lake, at the far end of which
you can see a shining figure standing. You start to walk
more quickly because you are impatient to see this
brilliant figure more closely.

When you finally reach the figure and can see it
in detail, you realise that it is an angel! Your heart is
beating loudly, although the figure does not seem to pay
any attention to you as it fills a small, shining cauldron
with water from the lake. This is the right time to greet
the angel. The smell of flowers becomes much stronger,
you can see his enormous wings and, although you do
not wish to interrupt him, you need to do so as soon as
possible. At this moment, the angel offers you a drink
from the cauldron, saying, 'You may drink the water.
It is pure. It is the water of life, of rejuvenation and
purification.'

After drinking, you look at the angel again and
experience a sense of wellbeing. Your mind is clear and
your body full of energy.

Contact using the angel cards

There are various ways of using the set of 72 angel cards that accompany this book.

The angel of your birth date

By consulting the chart below, you can use the month and day of your birth to locate the name of your special angel in the pack.

The procedure is simple. Let us take 24 May as an example of a birth date. Look for 24-05 in the second column from the left and look to the right to read the name of the angel that corresponds to that line, in this case, Manakel, who belongs to the angelic order of guardians. This is the angel who you should invoke or, additionally, for who you can place a talisman or offering on your altar, or whose card you can place there. Read about your angel in the next chapter.

06-01	20-03	01-06	13-08	25-10	Vehuiah	Seraphim
07-01	21-03	02-06	14-08	26-10	Jeliel	Seraphim
08-01	22-03	03-06	15-08	27-10	Sitael	Seraphim
09-01	23-03	04-06	16-08	28-10	Elemiah	Seraphim
10-01	24-03	05-06	17-08	29-10	Mahasiah	Seraphim
11-01	25-03	06-06	18-08	30-10	Lelahel	Seraphim
12-01	26-03	07-06	19-08	31-10	Achaiah	Seraphim
13-01	27-03	08-06	20-08	01-11	Cahetel	Seraphim
14-01	28-03	09-06	21-08	02-11	Haziel	Cherubim
15-01	29-03	10-06	22-08	03-11	Aladiah	Cherubim
16-01	30-03	11-06	23-08	04-11	Loviah	Cherubim
17-01	31-03	12-06	24-08	05-11	Ahaiah	Cherubim
18-01	01-04	13-06	25-08	06-11	Iezalel	Cherubim
19-01	02-04	14-06	26-08	07-11	Mebahel	Throne
20-01	03-04	15-06	27-08	08-11	Hariel	Throne
21-01	04-04	16-06	28-08	09-11	Hekamiah	Throne
22-01	05-04	17-06	29-08	10-11	Lauviah	Cherubim

					Name	Order
23-01	06-04	18-06	30-08	11-11	Caliel	Cherubim
24-01	07-04	19-06	31-08	12-11	Leuuiah	Cherubim
25-01	08-04	20-06	01-09	13-11	Pahaliah	Cherubim
26-01	09-04	21-06	02-09	14-11	Nelchael	Cherubim
27-01	10-04	22-06	03-09	15-11	Yeiayel	Cherubim
28-01	11-04	23-06	04-09	16-11	Melahel	Cherubim
29-01	12-04	24-06	05-09	17-11	Haheuiah	Cherubim
30-01	13-04	25-06	06-09	18-11	Nithaiah	Power
31-01	14-04	26-06	07-09	19-11	Haaiah	Power
01-02	15-04	27-06	08-09	20-11	Yeratel	Power
02-02	16-04	28-06	09-09	21-11	Seheiah	Power
03-02	17-04	29-06	10-09	22-11	Reiiel	Power
04-02	18-04	30-06	11-09	23-11	Omael	Power
05-02	19-04	01-07	12-09	24-11	Lecabel	Power
06-02	20-04	02-07	13-09	25-11	Vasairiah	Power
07-02	21-04	03-07	14-09	26-11	Yehudiah	Dominion
08-02	22-04	04-07	15-09	27-11	Lehahiah	Dominion
09-02	23-04	05-07	16-09	28-11	Chavakiah	Dominion
10-02	24-04	06-07	17-09	29-11	Menadel	Dominion
11-02	25-04	07-07	18-09	30-11	Aniel	Dominion
12-02	26-04	08-07	19-09	01-12	Haamiah	Dominion
13-02	27-04	09-07	20-09	02-12	Rehael	Dominion
14-02	28-04	10-07	21-09	03-12	Eiazel	Dominion
15-02	29-04	11-07	22-09	04-12	Hahahel	Principality
16-02	30-04	12-07	23-09	05-12	Mikael	Principality
17-02	01-05	13-07	24-09	06-12	Veuliah	Principality
18-02	02-05	14-07	25-09	07-12	Yelahiah	Principality
19-02	03-05	15-07	26-09	08-12	Saeliah	Principality
20-02	04-05	16-07	27-09	09-12	Ariel	Principality
21-02	05-05	17-07	28-09	10-12	Asaliah	Principality
22-02	06-05	18-07	29-09	11-12	Mihael	Principality
23-02	07-05	19-07	30-09	12-12	Vehuel	Archangel
24-02	08-05	20-07	01-10	13-12	Daniel	Archangel
25-02	09-05	21-07	02-10	14-12	Hahaziah	Archangel
26-02	10-05	22-07	03-10	15-12	Imamiah	Archangel
27-02	11-05	23-07	04-10	16-12	Nanael	Archangel
28-02	12-06	24-07	05-10	17-12	Nithael	Archangel
01-03	13-05	25-07	06-10	18-12	Mebahiah	Archangel
02-03	14-05	26-07	07-10	19-12	Poiel	Archangel
03-03	15-05	27-07	08-10	20-12	Nemamiah	Virtue

04-03	16-05	28-07	09-10	21-12	Ieilael	Virtue
05-03	17-05	29-07	10-10	22-12	Harael	Virtue
06-03	18-05	30-07	11-10	23-12	Mitzrael	Virtue
07-03	19-05	31-07	12-10	24-12	Umabel	Virtue
08-03	20-05	01-08	13-10	25-12	Iahhel	Virtue
09-03	21-05	02-08	14-10	26-12	Annauel	Virtue
10-03	22-05	03-08	15-10	27-12	Mehiel	Virtue
11-03	23-05	04-08	16-10	28-12	Damabiah	Guardian
12-03	24-05	05-08	17-10	29-12	Manakel	Guardian
13-03	25-05	06-08	18-10	30-12	Eiael	Guardian
14-03	26-05	07-08	19-10	31-12	Habuiah	Guardian
15-03	27-05	08-08	20-10	01-01	Rochel	Guardian
16-03	28-05	09-08	21-10	02-01	Gabamiah	Guardian
17-03	29-05	10-08	22-10	03-01	Haiaiel	Guardian
18-03	30-05	11-08	23-10	04-01	Mumiah	Guardian
19-03	31-05	12-08	24-10	05-01	Vehuiah	Seraphim

Choosing an angel card

1. Choose from the 72 cards associated with this book a picture of an angel that especially appeals to you.

2. Keep the card close to you for two weeks. Only when the angel has become part of you can you proceed to the next step. Do not try to find any special energy or celestial light yet.

3. Enter into contact with your angel. Imagine that you are standing close and let him take you to the required dimension.

4. Once you have reached the required dimension, you will see an entrance or a door appear before you.

5. Open the door and begin to ask the angel questions.

What to do next?

1. Ask the angel's advice about your problem.

2. Imagine the solution to your situation, whether it is physical or emotional or another type of problem.

3. Carefully observe all that comes into your mind.

4. If need be, ask for further details in order to solve your problem.

5. Thank the angel for his attention and advice.

An alternative

1. If you have a problem, talk to the angel about it and then listen to what he says.

2. Pay close attention, as the reply is often symbolic or esoteric in nature.

3. Continue to converse with the angel until you perceive that the solution is clear.

4. If you feel that you are still caught at a crossroads, ask the angel for a lesser solution, even if this does not solve your problem quickly.

See Chapter 3 for information on using the angel cards in other ways, and for detailed explanations of the characteristics of each angel in the pack.

Proclamations

A proclamation is a statement that is written and/or spoken out loud. It is intended to show belief in, and enthusiasm for, angels and what they are able to do. By proclaiming, we assert in a positive and hopeful sense that which we are asking for to be manifested in our reality. This shows our faith, so as to attract that which we believe and deserve. You can incorporate proclamations into your rituals, or use them separately.

The proclamation below can be used in a general situation, and the ones below that are suitable for a range of specific circumstances.

I proclaim infinite truth and love, that are to bring to me what I deserve by right of conscience.

I proclaim the joy of feeling the indescribable presence of the angels and, through them, bring to my body, mind and spirit, fulfilment without effort, happiness and material and spiritual wealth.

I proclaim my freedom in all senses, the expansion of my consciousness and success in all my projects and purposes.

So it is, for it has always been so, and because it will be so for ever.

Proclamation of prosperity and wealth

Prosperity and wealth come to me, flooding my life and my home with spiritual and material goods. Everything belongs to me and I belong to everything. Everyday I give more and receive more from life.

I invoke the celestial power and the angels so that success and opulence come to me in the shape and quantity that I desire.

Proclamation of abundance and sufficiency

Abundance and money come into my life to fill it sufficiently with all that is necessary. I feel in me the abundance and quality of life that money gives.

I invoke the celestial power and the angels so that my income and work will always be enough to fulfil my hopes.

Proclamation of good fortune

Good fortune always falls on me from Heaven. I am successful in all that I do and circumstances are always in my favour. I am creating new and brilliant hopes for my being and my personality.

I invoke the celestial power and the angels so that they keep me protected by the magic and power of the universe.

Proclamation of success in business

The power of creativity flows inside me and shows itself through my success in business. I attain the necessary funds at the right moment and the results are excellent. I invoke the celestial power and the angels so that my business continues to progress and success accompanies me on my adventure.

Proclamation of peace and harmony

I am surrounded by goodness, happiness and fulfilment without effort. Peace and harmony govern my life now and in any situation or place in which I find myself.

I invoke the celestial power and the angels so that they keep me in light and in a constant state of positive vibrations.

Proclamation of health and vitality

Health and vitality flow through me like a powerful spring of life-curing water that penetrates my body and the atmosphere of any place I find myself. The power of vitality comes towards me and makes me feel strong and vigorous.

I invoke the celestial power and the angels so that they keep us healthy in body, happy in spirit and full of life forever.

Proclamation of love

Love penetrates my whole being and the beings that I love, and return my feelings to the same measure. Our world is full of harmony.

I invoke the celestial power and the angels so that the perfume of love intoxicates our hearts and its violet light illuminates our souls.

Proclamation of passion

Passion intoxicates my being and that of the person I love, and who returns my feelings with the same measure. Our relationship is full of gratifying experiences.

I invoke the celestial power and the angels so that the perfume of love intoxicates our senses and its fragrance surrounds our lives with passion.

Proclamation for the protection of children

The guardian angels rejoice when children are healthy, happy and safe. To protect them is always their mission. My children are protected and guided by the wisdom and intelligence of the universe.

I invoke the celestial power and the angels so that my beloved children, sweet fruit of my heart, are always safe and protected.

Proclamation for the protection of a loved one

No circumstance, situation, place or person can go against the positive flow of life and destiny of whoever is part of my life and accompanies me on my path. Reality shows itself before them in a favourable way.

I invoke the celestial power and the angels so that my loved one is always accompanied by positive vibrations of light and security.

Invocations

Invocation means to call on in prayer. The purpose of making an invocation is to ask an angel to be with you and help you, often a particular angel for a specific mission. Here is a typical invocation:

> I, (here you should say your name), invoke you, Guardian Angel, for my good and the good of all humanity. I ask you and order you to give me the privilege of your undoubted presence for the Glory of God and as a testament of my faith in the angels. Thank you for what you are about to grant me.

If you wish, when petitioning your guardian angel or any angel, you could hold tightly in one hand a cross (or a crucifix) similar to the ones shown below. Choose a style that appeals to you the most or best represents your call for protection.

Invocation with crosses

Anchor cross:
protection at sea

Royal anchor cross:
protection on beaches

Celtic cross:
protection on plains

Calvary cross:
protection when meditating

Square cross:
when studying

Thorny cross:
protection in arguments

Greek cross:
protection at birth

Cross of Jerusalem:
protection from lack of faith

Latin cross:
protection when praying

Lorraine cross:
protection during operations

Maltese cross:
protection for sailors

Monograms of Christ:
protection from Satan

Papal cross:
protection from the impious

Patriarchal cross:
protection from evil relatives

Pommelled cross:
protection from heresy

Templar cross:
protection from aggression

Russian cross:
protection from the cold

Cross of the Holy Land:
protection from treachery

Other crosses   There are other crosses traditionally designated as protective in all kinds of situations. Some examples of the most important crosses (religious and otherwise) and their symbolism are listed below. You may like to incorporate ones appropriate to your own petitions to the angels.

- Inverted anchor cross: protection when fishing.
- Christian anchor cross: protection on warships.
- Catacomb cross: protection for the persecuted.
- Decusate cross: protection from doubt.
- Cross of St Anthony: protection from pain.
- Widened cross: protection in business.
- Coiled cross: protection from doubt.
- Fleur-de-Lys cross: protection in sobriety.
- Florentine cross: protection in the countryside.
- Swastika: protection at crossroads.
- New swastika: protection in uncertainty.
- India cross: protection in poverty.
- Justinian cross: protection in wealth.
- Cross with holes: protection from losing money.
- Pointed cross: protection from lightning.
- Radiant cross: protection from snow.
- Almond cross: protection from strong winds.
- Double cross: protection from avalanches.
- Winged cross: protection from bad harvests.

Powerful allies – the archangels

Below are some suggested visualisations and prayers for connecting with the four most powerful archangels, described in some detail in the previous chapter, and other archangels and angels.

Visualisation for the archangel Michael

Michael, I claim your golden angelic presence before me, to help me in _____ . Send your shining golden light; make it penetrate the crown chakra and expand through my whole body until it reaches my feet. I also invoke the presence of the angel protector of _____ (if you wish to ask the help of the angel protector for another person, put their birth date here) and am eternally grateful for your valuable help.

Visualisation for the archangel Raphael

In order to thank and make contact with this angel, you should first light a green candle and place a glass of water and three yellow flowers in it in the room.

Raphael, I invoke your violet and silver light that envelops and penetrates my whole body. I wish you to help me to achieve my dream of _____ because I know that you are my angel protector and you will achieve it.

I am grateful for your goodwill and for the gifts that will surely reach me, and I promise to faithfully follow your instructions.

If it is necessary, you can also ask the help of another angel. After having seen what you wish to happen as if it were on a television screen, and having thanked all the angels for their help, you can leave the meditation.

Visualisation for the archangel Gabriel

Before you start, light a pink candle, place three lilac flowers or three roses and a glass of water in the room. Don't forget to thank your angel protector for his divine intervention.

> *Gabriel, I invoke your shining lilac light and ask you to show yourself before me, to help me to _____ because you can do so as my angel protector. I am grateful for your goodwill and just balance; I invoke you so that you help me and I again thank you for your infinite love and goodwill.*

Visualisation for the archangel Uriel

The archangel Uriel can assist in bringing to the surface all those negative feelings and turning them into the energy of altruistic love. He can sharpen perception and healing powers, and help to awaken an understanding of being part of the whole. He is also the protector of children and the weak and destitute. The simple fact of making contact with this archangel can, little by little, change corporal and mental energy, opening up and calming the conscience.

If the petition is important, light a pink candle on nine consecutive days, and place a glass of water in the special place where you connect with the angels, and some flowers. Change the water every day and the flowers when they wilt.

> *I ask the archangel Uriel to present himself and send his pink, lilac and golden rays of love to me and help me to _____ I know that this is occurring at this moment and I am grateful for his help.*

Prayers to the archangel St Michael

1

Oh most glorious St Michael Archangel!
Prince and ruler of the celestial armies,
custodian and defender of souls,
guardian of the Church,
vanquisher, terror and fear of the rebel infernal spirits.
We humbly beg you to free from all evil
those who call on you with confidence.
That your favour should shelter us,
your fortress defend us and that, through your
    incomparable protection,
we move ever forward in the service of the Lord.
That your virtue gives us hope every day of our lives,
especially in the trance of death,
so that, defended by your power from the infernal
    dragon and all his traps,
when we leave this world we are presented by you,
free of all guilt, before the Divine majesty.
Amen.

2

St Michael Archangel, defend us in battle.
Be our shelter from the Devil.
God crush him, we beg,
and you, Prince of the Celestial Militia,
throw Satan into Hell with your divine power,
and the other evil spirits
that scattered walk the world
to the perdition of souls.
Amen.

3

St Michael Archangel, defend us in the struggle,
be our shelter from the perversity and traps of the Devil.
May God humble his pride.
And you, Prince of the Celestial Militia,
throw Satan into Hell with the evil spirits
that roam the world to the perdition of souls.
Amen.

Prayers to the archangel St Gabriel

1

Our Lord God,
We beg your mercy so that having known your
    Incarnation
by the announcement of the archangel Gabriel,
with his help we also receive his benefits.
For Jesus Christ our Lord.
Amen.

2

Oh God! Amongst all the angels, you chose the loving
    archangel St Gabriel
to announce the mystery of your Incarnation.
Gracefully give us that celebrate his festivity on Earth,
experience his patronage in Heaven
(Here you ask for that which you desire.)
Most powerful archangel St Gabriel,
you who are the force of God,
wash me in your blessed waters of purification,
raise my intuition, and help me to remember what I am.
In dreams give me the liquid of true love to drink.
And with trumpet announce to my soul
that it is now time to rise from amongst the dead
and resuscitate my consciousness in the Light.
Amen.

Prayers to St Raphael

1

Archangel St Raphael, you who said:
'Thank God each day and proclaim his goodness.
Do good and do not fall into evil.
Good is the prayer with fasting, and give alms before
counting gold.'
I beg you to accompany me on all my paths
and that you give me grace to follow your advice.
Amen.

2

Glorious archangel St Raphael, medicine of God,
you who guided Tobias on his journey,
you prepared him a happy marriage and gave back the
sight of his aged father,
guide us on the road to salvation,
cure our ills, help us in our need,
make our homes happy and give us the vision of God in
Heaven.
Most powerful archangel Saint Raphael, help me to
cure my thoughts,
to communicate well with my fellows
and to be an open channel for your curative force.
Lead me by the road of health of body and soul,
to be worthy of reaching total freedom and melting into
the light of God.
Amen.

Prayer to the archangel Uriel

Oh God! Who with indescribable providence
sends your holy angels to guard us,
accept our pleas and keep us always under your
    protection.
Lord, that confides us to your angels so that they guard
    us on all our paths,
let us by intervention of your glorious archangel
    St Uriel
see ourselves free of present danger,
and assure us against all adversity.
Glorious archangel St Uriel, powerful in spirit,
I implore your protection to gain victory against all
    spiritual or worldly evil.
My protector, give me the grace that I ask of you (here
    you ask the grace you desire),
if it is convenient for the good of my soul,
accompany me and guide all my steps until I reach
    eternal life.
Amen.

Prayer to Barachiel

Barachiel is often depicted carrying a basket or bunch
of flowers and precious fruit (the fruit of completed
vocation), and is sometimes in the form of a woman.
One's path in life, or vocation, is the area Barachiel can
help with. As St Paul said: 'I exhort you to walk with
dignity in your vocation, that has been given to you,
with all humility, sweetness and patience'.

We ask St Barachiel to keep us from falling into idleness,
from indifference to Holy things, from the mortal half-
    heartedness,
and to free the souls that we pray for, or that surround us,
of the capital sin of idleness
and the mortal fall into lies and indifference.

The archangel Jehudiel is our guide and help in cases
of envy and jealousy. His unconditional acceptance of
the Divine Decree and his zeal in carrying out his duties
seal his eternal alliance with God. He glorifies and
exalts love, altruism, and the glory of God. We should
ask him to keep us from falling into envy and jealousy,
which destroy the peace of the soul, that he protect us
from people obsessed by jealousy and the persistent evil
of envy.

Holy archangel Jehudiel, powerful angel and great
    opponent of evil spirits,
come to our help with your angelic army.
Assist us in the fight against envy and the tremendous
    attacks of Hell,
which threatens to destroy the peace of families.
Remove all evil from our hearts.

Prayer to Jehudiel

The archangel Saethiel is usually depicted with his
hands together in deep prayer, signifying his joyful
union with God. He fights the spirit of gluttony,
excessive drinking and other things taken to excess.
Saethiel can help to hold us back from our own
incontrollable impulses, or to place limits on people in
our house or those we know who wish to do us harm.
He can also mitigate the sin of gluttony, changing it
into true enjoyment of food and therefore giving us
better health.

    As a giver of grace, he carries a bunch of flowers (or
even fruit), or scatters flowers and fruit, inciting people
to enjoy life. Happiness, especially that of children, is

Prayer to Saethiel

important to Saethiel and he is considered by many to be their guardian angel. The knowledge that they are protected by the father-like goodness of this angel helps them to remain calm in potentially dangerous circumstances. He can also be invoked when families suffer from discord or continuous infidelity.

Holy archangel Saethiel! Help us with your angels, teach us to pray, as God has prayed and has taught us to pray!

Amen.

God also has a multitude of celestial beings under his control who help Him to bestow new knowledge, as well as wisdom, upon humans. These angels are especially gifted in philosophical matters, in science and occasionally in magic. Their presence is always welcomed and nobody who wishes to become a grand master of anything can do without them. Among others, they include: Dorothiel (concerned with the correct execution of contracts and legacies); Raysel (intervenes in all things related to money and its exchange); Baruchas (intervenes to improve and boost relations between master and servant, bosses and employees); Amadiel (the angel of love, the same way as Cupid; he is considered eternally in love and works to unite couples, although he is infuriated by adultery or infidelity); Symiel (the celestial policeman who watches over and judges the actions of humans, so no evil person can escape the consequences of what they have done; he is a friend of the military and, in general, of any person in uniform).

Connecting with a guardian angel

The following meditation is simple and effective, and through it you can come to know the name of your guardian angel. It is written as if from a guardian angel himself.

Meditation

Every day there is a thought from me to you, and a space for you to tell me something if you so desire; I will be waiting with the greatest love whenever you wish to do so, but I will equally be greatly happy at the times when you do not wish to write to me.

I would like you to know my name. I will send it to you through a simple meditation (it is better that you do this at night, before going to sleep).

You should be relaxed and be secure in the knowledge that I will communicate with you. If you do not hear my name during the exercise, you will know it one morning when you awaken. It could be the morning after the meditation, it all depends upon your openness towards me.

When I finish this letter, I will describe to you the exercise and, once you know it, you can write my name in your diary after every message from me to you. You can also call me by my name always.

The name that you will hear or receive mentally is the one that I wish you to call me by. I tell you this because many people wait to hear a Biblical name or one that sounds different from their language, but it is not always so. We use simple names. The vibration of my name will produce positive effects in you. I will be grateful if you use my name.

Did you know that, when you received your name, it was whispered by me? It has a vibration that unites us more. Each time that you wish to talk with me, you can. I am always by your side and, now that you begin to think of me, the light that you project towards me will open space and bring me closer. Your own light and mine will illuminate you and I will cover you with my wings so that you remain forever within my aura.

Always remember that I love you with the deepest love and that, today, all the angels celebrate this great event and wish to transmit this message: 'We are your friends, we love you and you only need to call us for us to come flying to your help'. Now, try to feel all the love that all we angels are sending you. I have always waited for this moment and, today, when you approach me, I rejoice and my soul shines more brightly. All the angels are rejoicing and I firmly embrace you so as to guide you with love, because I love you.

Now, to hear my name, you only have to relax, be calm and listen with your heart. First, breathe deeply three times and, whilst you do so, think that you are inhaling fresh, golden light that emanates from my angelical heart. I embrace you with profound love, I hold you to me. Now, think that you are seeing many angels that bring you the smell of the countryside and bathe you with the most subtle essences. You are shining and happy, now I whisper you my name, listen with your heart. I love you deeply. I am your guardian angel and my name is _____.

You can say or sing the following hymns and prayers during your ritual or any other time of the day or night.

Holy guardian angel, companion of my life,
you who never leaves me, neither day or night.
Although spirit invisible, you are by my side,
listening to my prayers, with me you reside.
In the shadows of the night, the demon you withhold,
covering my breast with wings of pearl and gold.
Angel of God, I hear the message you send,
May I go with you to God in the end.
Witness of the invisible, presence from Heaven my
    friend,
I thank you for the protection that you lend.
In the presence of angels we sing our song,
Glory to the Father, Holy Ghost and Son.

Amen.

Hymn to a guardian angel

I (your name) invoke you, divine guardian angel,
so that you fulfil the destiny that God gave you and that
    you protect me.
I hope that very soon the light descends on me and on
    my home.
Your presence will be a balm in my life.

Invocation of the guardian angel

Prayers to a guardian angel

1

Holy angel, my celestial guide,
who so many times I have saddened with my sins,
do not abandon me. I beg of you.
In the midst of danger, do not remove your support.
Do not lose me from sight for an instant,
but let your friendly inspiration guide and fortify
    my soul,

revive my faint and almost stopped heart,
because it is without love.
Send it some spark from the soft and pure flames that
    burn you,
so that when the end of this life comes I can,
in your company and that of all the angels,
obtain eternal life and see Jesus without cease, love him,
    praise him and bless him.
Amen.

2

Holy angel, I implore you to accompany me day and
    night,
so that you are by my side helping me in the difficult
    moments and increasing my
happiness in moments of fortune.
If all human beings have the shelter of an angel,
I too wish to enjoy this privilege.
I choose you because you are a being full of light.
I choose you because you are invested with the power
    of God
and because I am captivated by your name in which
    your power rests.
Holy angel, walk by my side, the same as my shadow,
be my companion, let your light fall on me and light
    my way.
I (your name) name you (name of the angel) as my
    angel protector.
Amen.

Holy Angel, loved by God,   **3**
who after taking me, by divine orders, under your
    blessed protection,
never do you cease to defend, illuminate and guide me.
I venerate you as my protector, I love you as my guard;
I submit to your rule and give myself to you, to be
    governed by you.
So I beg you and by the love of Jesus Christ I plead,
that when I am ungrateful to you and obstinately deaf
    to your inspiration,
you do not, however, abandon me;
before this, the opposite, place me on the right path, if
    I have strayed from it.
Teach me, if I am ignorant;
raise me up, if I have fallen;
support me, if I am in danger,
and lead me to Heaven so I have there eternal happiness.
Amen.

Angel of peace, guardian angel, to whom I am entrusted,   **4**
my defender, my vigilant sentinel.
I give you thanks, that you freed me from much harm to
    body and spirit.
I give you thanks, that while I slept, you watched me,
    and awake, you led me;
in my ear, with holy inspiration you advised me.
Forgive me, my friend, messenger of Heaven, advisor,
    protector and my faithful guardian.
Strong wall of my soul, defender and celestial
    companion.
In my disobedience, vileness and discourtesy,
help me and guard me always, by night and day.
Amen.

Some more prayers to angels

Apart from your guardian angel, the archangels and the 72 angels in the accompanying pack, in order to ask for something specific, you can invoke other angels that have special abilities in a certain field. The responses these angels give allow you to communicate with your inner self, covering a wide range of aspects on a spiritual and intuitive level.

Invocation of the angels of the four elements

Lord God Almighty, creator of heaven and earth
Clement and merciful Lord,
send me your four angels:
the angel of earth, the angel of water, the angel of air
    and the angel of fire,
so that your will is manifested in me.

The angel of earth comes to collect all the waste of my
    physical body,
he absorbs it and returns it to me in the shape of health
    and purity.
Clean my whole body
so that my life can circulate fluidly through my veins
    and arteries.
It lightens, liberates and eases my whole being, and the
    kingdom of God and its justice
become reality on earth, and the golden age appears
    amongst humans.

The angel of water comes to wash all stains from my heart.
Selfless love nests in my heart and brings me happiness, fortune and joy.
My heart is clean, crystalline, transparent, and the kingdom of God and its justice
become reality on earth, and the golden age appears amongst humans.

The angel of fire, which is no other than the angel of the sun,
comes to sanctify my soul and my spirit.
The absolute truth enters my whole being.
My soul and my spirit know eternal life and are the dwelling of creative divine omnipotence, and the kingdom of God and its justice become reality on earth, and the golden age appears amongst humans.
And so it is for the glory of God and His justice. So it is for the glory of God.

Amen.

Invocation of good angels

Oh, you benevolent and glorious angels!
Urzla, Zlar, Larzod and Arzal, I invoke you.
I beg you to visibly appear in the name of God.
Bestow on me useful virtues and power so that I can achieve my wishes.
Therefore, now I seriously and powerfully implore you,
Oh, good angels Urzla, Zlar, Larzod and Arzal, in the name of God,
so that you show me the crystal stone before me.
And that through said stone you transmit your ray to my sight and your voice to my ears, so that I can hear you and that you give me all the mysteries that I seriously beg of you.

Oh, good and friendly angels!
I as a servant of the Almighty invoke you so that you
    become visible now before me.
Oh, servants of mercy, come and show yourselves
    before me
and allow me to share the confidential wisdom of your
    Creator.
Amen.

Invocation of the archangels

Michael, Michael, Michael, prince of the archangels,
out of all the grateful hearts spring songs of praise.
All on earth adore you for your celestial presence.
God that comes from the sun with all that the name
    implies.

Michael, Michael, Michael, let the guardian angels of
    your celestial legions
come to liberate us all.
Purify, illuminate and manifest the glory of the
    perfection of the light that reaches us.

Jofiel and Chamuel, Gabriel and Raphael, Uriel and
    Zadkiel and powerful hosts of light.
Cherubim and seraphim of the kingdoms of glory,
tear away the veil that blinds our human vision.
Blessed seven archangels, we ask you for illumination,
we invoke your presence in hymns to your praise.
Keep us consecrated in the completion of God's plan so
    as to be, with purity,
your ministers.
Amen.

The Power of the Angels Cards

This chapter centres on the 72 angels depicted on the numbered cards in the accompanying set, and outlines some ways to use them to interpret both the present and the future. Within each angel's individual qualities, traditional attributes and the symbology of the cards lies the answer to what the reader seeks to know or understand. The angels are a luminous consciousness that show the path we must follow in order to discover the angelic qualities of our own natures, to uncover the wisdom and power each of us possesses.

These cards are based on the angels of the Kabbalah, which is a Jewish oral, mystical tradition that developed over many hundreds of years alongside the Torah (the first five books of the Old Testament – Genesis, Exodus, Leviticus, Numbers and Deuteronomy). A rich and complex seam of Judaic theology which has become very popular in our own times, the Kabbalah is a way, a system, of seeking to understanding how God works, especially through hidden meanings in words. Angels are an important part of the Kabbalic view of the cosmos, which holds that they are divine energies around, and guiding, us all the time.

The basic concept behind the angel cards is that we take our problem (of energy which shows itself in a negative way) to a higher dimension with a superior vibration – that is, an angel – in the hope and expectation that interaction with this higher vibration will help resolve the problem. The vehicle for this journey to another dimension (place) in a higher octave (vibration) is our imagination. Imagination or guided visualisation allows us to tap into particular energy patterns and when these visualisation techniques are combined with Kabbalistic information related to the angel cards, a higher plane can be reached. Hopefully, we will be enabled to see our lives holistically, in their entirety, the interconnections of everything, including the areas of love, work, relationships and social life, health and finances.

Divining the way to proceed and the future through the angels is one of the best options for clarifying our dilemmas. Making contact with these divine entities who also have knowledge of our human condition means our problems are always familiar to them. The angels do not seek our devotion or thanks – although they deserve it – and it is in this selfless help that their strength lies.

Using the angel cards

The previous chapter suggested consulting the angel cards through knowledge of the angel (see the relevant description in this chapter for each numbered angel) connected to your date of birth, and also by choosing single cards and incorporating them into your rituals.

Another way of using the cards is to spread out all the cards face-down on the table at the start of a session. Then, after some minutes, extract one card. The angel on its face will be the custodian of the session. Next, shuffle the remaining cards and spread them out, face-down again. Using the left hand, extract one or more depending on the ritual desired. Reveal what these cards are.

Now comes the moment of meditation, of focusing inwardly, aiming to connect with the angel/s on the card/s. Close your eyes and let them make contact – something that they will certainly do as their power is fast and free of intermediaries and permission. There is no risk of their harming us or not wanting to appear, the only requirement is to strongly believe in them as an act of faith and to speak to them from the heart. There could be occasions you see a vibrant colour or smell the subtle aroma of incense. There is also the possibility that the room will become quieter and pervaded by almost imperceptible music.

After some time spent focusing on the qualities and attributes of the particular angel/s, ask questions mentally or out loud, on your own behalf or that of another person.

The type of draw depends on the complexity of the problem, as shown below.

1. The simple draw: a problem is posed, a card is taken and it is interpreted.

2. Past, present and future draw: the same as before but each question refers to a moment in our lives (past, present and future).

PAST   PRESENT   FUTURE

3. Complex draw: if a very complex question is posed, many cards are picked at random and interpretations are attempted until what they are saying is understood.

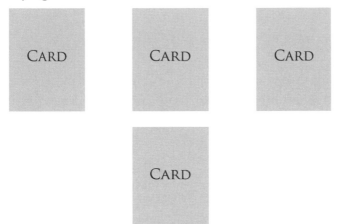

   Depending on the difficulties encountered or the complexity of the problem, a maximum of ten cards can be chosen – the same number as the Ten Commandments. According to the numbers, place the cards in groups of three with the last card placed below. The task is now to apply what the cards tell you (or the person for whom you are reading the cards) to an aspect of your own life (or the life of the other person). Note: The interpretation of what is being told by the card differs according to whether the chosen card is looked at right way up or upside down.

- This ritual with the cards must be carried out in a private place where you will not be interrupted, especially by children.

Follow these rules

- A positive mental state must be maintained throughout the ritual. Imagine that what you are asking for is being carried out.

- Only light the candles with wooden matches. Candles must not be put out by blowing but by using a dampened thumb and index finger, or a snuffer.

- Wash your hands after finishing the ritual. If possible, change out of the clothes worn during the ritual and wash them.

Take into account

- The angels will not show their presence if the ritual is carried out frivolously, faithlessly or to satisfy curiosity.

- It is only in exceptional cases that the angels show themselves in bodily form to humans.

- Angels often reveal their presence in symbolic ways. Be very attentive to signals and pay attention to dreams; watch out particularly for strangers who say something important or spiritual.

- Try to interpret the angelic message when you receive an unexpected gift or small personal objects disappear and then later reappear.

About the angel cards

On the following pages, the characteristics and attributes of the angels of each of the 72 cards are described, and other details are provided, including the hierarchy to which each angel belongs (identified by the colour of the frame around their image). All this information is provided to enable you to better connect with the angel. As mentioned previously, although the angels are here referred to as 'he/him', angels are not really considered to be either male or female, and what is said should be interpreted as describing both male and female beings and applying to male and female card-readers.

Visual representation of angels varies depending on the culture and religion to which the artist belongs. In Europe, the first pictures of angels were crudely executed by Christian artists of the forth and fifth centuries; when, around a thousand years later, artists of great talent and sensitivity, such as Angelico, Giotto, Rafael, Michelangelo and Correggio, painted angels they created works of art of immense beauty.

The images of the 72 different angels in the deck of angel cards associated with this book were inspired by the iconography of the Judeo-Christian tradition, but they were also influenced by the Hindu tradition of the angels of 'karma'. Karma comes from the word karmen which means 'to make', meaning that all human actions necessarily have consequences. According to this cosmic law of cause and effect, we are responsible for our own luck or ill fortune, but often we do not realise this and put the cause of our unhappiness down to external factors. With their combination of influences, the cards help us to see that we need to take responsibility for our lives and not blame others or circumstances for the way we are. Like the angels, we need to learn to love everyone, including ourselves.

1. VEHUIAH

Right way up

He has great protection on the astral level and is on earth to be the precursor to a new world. His interests lie in the most diverse issues. Extremely curious, balanced and optimistic, he is always seeking the truth. He faces everything with optimism, is well-mannered, and enjoys life best when his family is completely united. Blessed with a subtle spirituality and great astuteness, he is inventive and creative, an inspired artist. His gifts in writing and speaking may lead to an involvement in politics. His work will be rewarded and recognised.

Upside down

He has a tendency to have many loves. He enjoys social life, and with his magnetism and charisma mixes easily and is well accepted. He has a taste for competition and challenge, and often disputes the outcomes, although with generosity of spirit. He understands that difficult times occur so that there can be growth.

1. VEHUIAH

1 Vehuiah 1

Attribute: God raised above all things.

Planet: Neptune.

Angelic choir: Seraphim.

Ruling hour: From 12 am to 12.20 am.

Reasons for invoking:

To start up and carry out difficult things.

To become a warrior of spiritual fire.

2. JELIEL

Right way up

He likes to do everything quickly. When young he generally lacked the patience to listen to his teachers because he felt that he knew what they were going to tell him. He also knew from an early age that he is on earth for a reason and that his intuition will tell him what is right and what is wrong. He delights in truth and universal brotherly love, including helping his family, with whom he feels a karmic connection. His higher emotions are so well developed that through them he makes contact with his ruling angel.

Upside down

He never succumbs to negative influences and is so competent he can master any type of circumstance. Others see him as quite magical thanks to the good humour with which he resolves all situations. A bringer of peace where there is conflict, he defends truth and detests violence. He adores animals, flowers and all nature. A little vain, he always likes to be fashionable.

2. JELIEL

2   Jeliel   2

Attribute: God who provides aid.

Planet: Neptune.

Angelic choir: Seraphim.

Ruling hour: From 12.20 am to 12.40 am.

Reasons for invoking:

To achieve victory over those who attack us unjustly.

To calm popular uprisings and improve the
behaviour of governments.

To re-establish peace and fidelity between husbands and wives.

To re-establish harmony between employers and employees.

3. SITAEL

Right way up

He is good inside and out, a lofty soul whose strong charisma attracts favourable attention. He is aware of his good luck and the strong possibility of financial success. Always active, he breathes life, and lives each day in his own special way. His pride does not allow him to ask favours of anybody. Although a lone worker, he has many friends, to whom he generally gives accurate advice as he possesses good judgement and has a wide understanding of situations. He generally forgives those who try to do him wrong. Sometimes he appears a little inhibited for no reason.

Upside down

Kind, understanding and gentle, he is a great transformer, protecting and giving people incentive for coming up with new ideas. He likes parties, banquets and celebrations, although in his dress he is reserved. He says what he thinks as he does not know how to hide his feelings. He has many memories of things which were not lived in this incarnation, and which normally appear as dreams. His soul's aim is to be noble.

Attribute: God who gives hope to all creatures.

Planet: Neptune.

Angelic choir: Seraphim.

Ruling hour: From 12.40 am to 1 am.

Reasons for invoking:

To keep us calm in the face of adversity.

To protect from car accidents, muggings and other attacks.

To give us strength and will in our commitments.

4. ELEMIAH

Right way up

He is confident about his divine potential and set out to discover his gifts from a young age. Blessed with great charisma, he acts on intuition, especially his strong feelings when something is about to happen. He has great potential in his hands for healing and is always working on several projects at the same time. He loves opening the minds of others to new proposals and ideas, and is keen to help people, particularly those most in need. He never refuses a call although he sometimes feels a little sad when those he loves well abuse their good luck.

Upside down

Explanations of, and solutions to, the problems of this life come to him unconsciously, with no need to look for someone to help. He discovers what he believes in and how he wants to live through philosophy. He is interested in understanding primitive societies through anthropology and archaeology.

4   Elemiah   4

Attribute: Occult god.

Planet: Neptune.

Angelic choir: Seraphim.

Ruling hour: From 1 am to 1.20 am.

Reasons for invoking:

To calm us when facing adversity.

For protection on journeys.

For help in recognising traitors.

To help us to discover our profession.

To show us the error of our ways.

5. MAHASIAH

Right way up

He is an example of virtue and spirituality and his aura is clearly visible. Blessed with great internal balance, a sense of justice, generosity and wisdom, he acts within social or human laws. He learns everything easily and quickly – especially languages – as he remembers past lives. He is always growing and changing in various areas including work and his love life.

Upside down

He works well in esoteric ceremonies, and is able to summon spiritual forces and communicate with angels. He likes to spend time in meditation centres, conferences, congresses and spiritual seminars but always maintains his own integrity and awareness. He exclusively serves his truth, which is that of his God. He has tendencies to live in a sumptuous way, wanting to enlarge his house and to fill it with flowers and symbolic objects. He will probably have a sizeable library.

5   Mahasiah   5

Attribute: God the saviour.

Planet: Neptune.

Angelic choir: Seraphim.

Ruling hour: From 1.20 am to 1.40 am.

Reasons for invoking:

To live in peace with everyone.

To gain moral strength.

To grant us knowledge of the
sciences of the spirit.

To understand philosophy and theology.

6. LELAHEL

Right way up

Blessed with great idealism and balance, he has the strength to prevent evil. Always quick to help people in need, he makes sacrifices through acting without self-interest. He can sometimes lack willpower and it is possible for him to leave the battleground, although he tries to be master of himself. The symbol with which he is associated is the snake that bites its own tail as a symbol of rebirth. He feels the protection of God and the angelic world and is able to make strong psychic contact. He receives messages by tuning into the world of the spirits and he can even move objects through the power of the mind. He is able to develop concepts sent to him from an astral plane and simplify knowledge he has obtained from study of traditional texts so that more people can understand the beauty of the sciences of the angels.

Upside down

He uses his knowledge for great causes, his particular concerns being quality of life, awareness, and the state of humanity. He has ideas for building hospitals to help people, and for spiritual treatments, such as the use of crystals.

6   **Lelahel**   **6**

Attribute: Praiseworthy god.

Planet: Neptune.

Angelic choir: Seraphim.

Ruling hour: From 1.40 am to 2 am.

Reasons for invoking:

To cure illnesses of spirit.

To help us avoid being over-ambitious or
using power for illicit ends.

To help us reflect.

To protect us from wicked people.

7. ACHAIAH

Right way up

Of evolved appearance, he is highly spiritual but also has his feet on the ground. He looks to the horizon but has the stars on his mind. Although he may not have a formal education, he acquires knowledge that makes him influential. He always looks for the opportunities that life presents and intuitively knows how to deal with risks and avoid danger.

Upside down

He is obstinate and tenacious and possesses a great ability to see all points of view in different situations. Altruistic, immensely patient and understanding, he takes an interest in communicating with nature, using ultra-sensitive equipment or through the potential of the human brain.

7. ACHAIAH

7   Achaiah   7

Attribute: God of patience.

Planet: Neptune.

Angelic choir: Seraphim.

Ruling hour: From 2 am to 2.20 am.

Reasons for invoking:

To spread new ideas.

To make us capable of being patient.

To find sense in life when faith is lost.

To ask for help in order to succeed with difficult tasks.

To help us to discover the secrets of nature.

8. CAHETEL

Right way up

He has a harmonious character, balancing the spiritual with the material. He is mature and masters his impulses; due to his maturity, however, he sometimes feels disconnected from his social group, family and friends. He has a clear view of the world and its laws and always goes the furthest he can in what he proposes to do. He follows his heart and, with great intuition, shows humility in transmitting his knowledge and wisdom.

Upside down

He could be a pioneer in agricultural production. Although his success could be put down to luck, he knows how to share wealth with those closest to him. He always thanks God for everything he achieves.

8   Cahetel   8

Attribute: Adorable god.

Planet: Neptune.

Angelic choir: Seraphim.

Ruling hour: From 2.20 am to 2.40 am.

Reasons for invoking:

To protect people and things.

To expel 'evil spirits' or obsessive
negative thoughts.

To obtain God's compassion and blessing.

To favour agricultural production.

9. HAZIEL

Right way up

He has the grace and compassion of God because he understands rather than judges the mistakes of others. He appreciates that painful experiences occur so that we can move forward in our evolution. He enjoys the protection of older or influential people and, due to his brilliant performance, he often holds important posts. In the most difficult moments, he relies on Divine Providence and feels favoured in issues related to justice. A loyal companion and great friend, he has a nobility of character.

Upside down

He grows continually and knows that, despite obstacles, he will always achieve a deserved victory in any situation. He forgives even the gravest offences, knowing how to change the negative to positive. He does not lack effort in pursuit of his ideals.

Attribute: God of compassion.

Planet: Uranus.

Angelic choir: Cherubim.

Ruling hour: From 2.40 am to 3 am.

Reasons for invoking:

To give and receive goodwill.

To keep promises.

To receive support from others and divine compassion.

To have good friendships.

For reconciliation.

10. ALADIAH

Right way up

He is like an angel on earth –
understanding, reserved, and dedicated
to the person he loves. He has a vivid
imagination, self-confidence, flexibility
and an ability to always choose the best
paths to follow and moments to act.
Reliable and good-hearted, he is correct
in his manner of doing things. He has a
lively social life and mixes with the best
of society.

Upside down

A tireless worker, he will not hold
back on effort in order to achieve
a fairer society. He brings harmony,
and appreciates the need to look after
the body.

10 Aladiah 10

Attribute: Opportune god.

Planet: Uranus.

Angelic choir: Cherubim

Ruling hour: From 3 am to 3.20 am.

Reasons for invoking:

To heal physical and spiritual pains.

To protect us from poisonous psychic energies and jealousy.

To receive forgiveness when truly repentant.

To regenerate morale.

To enjoy the friendship of important people.

11. LOVIAH

Right way up

He is very inventive, developing ideas and applying them in a practical way, day to day. He is celebrated for his actions, enhancing his personality with each new experience in life. He has strong, lasting feelings for the people with whom he relates, and an immense capacity for love.

Upside down

With a passion for philosophy, he easily understands the world around him and is able to make excellent contact with others. He will face up to great challenges.

11   Loviah   11

Attribute: Exalted god.

Planet: Uranus.

Angelic choir: Cherubim.

Ruling hour: From 3.20 am to 3.40 am.

Reasons for invoking: To foresee outbreaks of nerves.

To protect against storms and lightning bolts.

To protect against pride and slander.

To defeat adversaries and overcome our weaknesses.

To rebuild friendships.

To protect us from fraud.

12. AHAIAH

Right way up

He is a living example – through his actions – of harmony with universal laws. Possessing a strong, wise, spiritual and discreet personality, his happiness comes from within. Serene, mature and balanced, his mission on earth is to enable others to discover their own spirituality. With deep brotherly feeling, he cares for those who have been abandoned, or who need good advice or calming when they are nervous.

Upside down

He is successful in things connected with the esoteric, as magic comes naturally to him. He can see people's auras and leans towards oriental knowledge. He is blessed with enormous charisma.

12   Ahaiah   12

Attribute: God of shelter.

Planet: Uranus.

Angelic choir: Cherubim.

Ruling hour: From 3.40 am to 4 am.

Reasons for invoking:

To interpret dreams and occult mysteries.

To provide help in general adversity.

To protect us from lies and abuse of trust.

To give us revelations, especially
about cosmology.

13. IEZALEL

Right way up

Knowledgeable about material and spiritual laws, he is the bearer of good news. The nobility of his character and dignity in his behaviour characterise his way of life. He is the centre of attraction in any environment due to three outstanding features: his wisdom, serenity and intuition. He often has the strong impression that he has already experienced – in another realm or life – what he is living now. He has a great capacity to adapt, and the purpose of his life is to transmute the crude into the spiritual. He only likes to put his time and effort into things that will come to something.

Upside down

This angel shows great knowledge in connection with other lives, and is thus able to help others in need. He has a gift of speaking, and possesses clear judgement.

13   Iezalel   13

Attribute: Glorified god.

Planet: Uranus.

Angelic choir: Cherubim.

Ruling hour: From 4 am to 4.20 am.

Reasons for invoking:

To obtain justice.

To free us from depression.

To protect against lies and false testimony.

To protect the innocent and let the
truth be known.

14. MEBAHEL

Right way up

He is a code-breaker of dreams, knowledgeable about material and spiritual laws. Always positive and confident, he is an urban defender, especially of the interests of the innocent. His ego shows a strong presence of spirit; highly adaptable, he strives constantly for spiritual regeneration. He lives out noble intentions and behaves with dignity in all situations, although he gets impatient about things that do not matter. His good sense, calm nature and insights gain him favour in all the spheres of his life.

Upside down

This angel imparts great knowledge and shows the legacy of other incarnations, to be used to assist those who need help. He is gifted in speaking and has sound judgement.

14. MEBAHEL

14 Mebahel 14

Attribute: Conservative god.

Planet: Saturn.

Angelic choir: Thrones.

Ruling hour: From 4.20 am to 4.40 am.

Reasons for invoking:

To ask for impartial judgements.

For protection against those who seek to pervert the good intentions of others.

To free us from negative attitudes.

15. HARIEL

Right way up

His religious faith is of a high order and he receives great illumination of which he is consciously aware. He has authority and extraordinary analytical intelligence, and the power to invoke magic and combat materialism in order to improve human existence. Pure in feeling, he has simple but refined material and social values. He sets up rites and customs in order to contribute to the expansion of spirituality, and organises associations, promotes conferences and works to bring about the legalisation of esoteric or alternative activities. Possessing a strong sense of justice, he always finds the path he needs to follow.

Upside down

As a realist, he always has his feet on the ground. He finds it easy to learn, create and study. He is always in a good mood, showing how life is simple and that we do not need to make it difficult. He always asks for things which will be granted quickly. A year of his life can be compared to five of another.

15. HARIEL

15   **Hariel**   15

Attribute: Creative god.

Planet: Saturn.

Angelic choir: Thrones.

Ruling hour: From 4.40 am to 5 am.

Reasons for invoking:

To obtain improvements in professional life.

To attract the love and goodwill of those
about us, especially among family members.

To exalt religious feelings.

To help us discover the useful and new.

16. HEKAMIAH

Right way up

He has a natural aura of peace, and his sincerity is reflected through his nobleness, authority, personality and prestige. He is true to his word, his character is frank, loyal, brave and upholds what he believes in. He looks out for his family and children, giving them priority over everything. Loved by all, he is respected for his sensitivity. He lives every minute of his life with much tenderness, love and hope, and wants everyone to have as honourable a life as his.

Upside down

He likes to be always changing things. Highly sensual, he enjoys tokens of his loves as a reminder of feelings from the past.

16. HEKAMIAH

16   Hekamiah   16

Attribute: God who creates the universe.

Planet: Saturn.

Angelic choir: Thrones.

Ruling hour: From 5 am to 5.20 am.

Reasons for invoking:

To help us transcend our problems.

To defeat our internal enemies.

To protect those in positions of leadership.

To ask for courage, perseverance and constancy.

17. LAUVIAH

Right way up

He has the ability to understand symbolic revelations and messages. The astral world shows itself through his unconscious, with visions, premonitions or images of higher worlds. His psychic faculties find expression in music, poetry, literature or philosophy. Through his noble character, his spirit radiates a very intense light. He knows that he is capable of achieving everything he wants to, mainly when what is required has been asked for by someone else. His dreams become reality.

Upside down

He reacts cordially and agreeably, comforting those close to him. He understands sadness as he knows the internal workings of human beings. Cultured, he likes the Kabbalah and philosophy.

17   Lauviah   17

Attribute: Admirable god.

Planet: Uranus.

Angelic choir: Cherubim.

Ruling hour: From 5.20 am to 5.40 am.

Reasons for invoking: To form deep friendships.

To show us the meaning of our dreams.

To develop artistic and literary talent.

To help us escape spiritual torment and sadness.

To sleep well.

To understand the spiritual sciences.

18. CALIEL

Right way up

He is intelligent, irreverent and charismatic, with strong personal magnetism. He has extraordinary intuition, especially when trying to discover the truth; often he only has to look in order to identify somebody's real intention. He possesses astuteness, patience and perseverance, analysing situations coolly and objectively in full detail. Incorruptible, he loves justice, truth and integrity and abhors laziness or the abstract.

Upside down

His logic is unquestionable and he is a true wizard who works miracles through his intense faith.

18. CALIEL

18   Caliel   18

Attribute: God who listens.

Planet: Uranus.

Angelic choir: Cherubim.

Ruling hour: From 5.40 am to 6 am.

Reasons for invoking:

To find a good defence counsel
in legal cases.

To provide help so that the truth
will come out in cases of conflict.

19. LEUUIAH

Right way up

He is friendly, jovial and modest in his words and ways. He bears all adversity with patience and resignation because he knows that this is a form of material and spiritual evolution. Extremely curious, he is ready to learn from any and all experiences.

Upside down

He is culturally refined and loves music, poetry and the arts in general. He has protection against adversaries or those who try to do him harm. This protection is a great wall of celestial light, invisible to the eyes of everyday people. He has complete dominion over the events of his life and receives the grace of God, maintaining a firm and decided stance in the fight for his ideals.

19   Leuuiah   19

Attribute: God who comes to the
aid of sinners.

Planet: Uranus.

Angelic choir: Cherubim.

Ruling hour: From 6 am to 6.20 am.

Reasons for invoking:

To bring us poetic and artistic inspiration.

To grant us divine grace in fertility.

To improve our memory and intelligence.

20. PAHALIAH

Right way up

Having developed a strong personality from a young age, he is a real custodian of justice, fighting for great ideals. He is extremely optimistic, a master of the art of discerning, and he likes to live in peace with others. He experiences in this life things which he had in another, mainly linked to family and children. He does not know how to live alone, needing a faithful companion in order to be happy. He generally appears younger than his real age. He feels comfortable in any situation.

Upside down

He studies the Kabbalah and understands that the invisible world can bring harmony to the visible world. He also studies other various topics in great depth.

Attribute: God of redemption.

Planet: Uranus.

Angelic choir: Cherubim.

Ruling hour: From 6.20 am to 6.40 am.

Reasons for invoking:

To give us revelations of truth and wisdom.

To help us find the right vocation.

21. NELCHAEL

Right way up

He can seem severe but shows moderation in words and achieves a balance between the spiritual and the material, loving the beautiful and hating the ugly and vulgar. He has a strong capacity for leadership, self-control and patience. He follows his ideal at any price, never accepting loss. Blessed with intelligence and imagination, he has maturity and control over himself. He seeks harmony among those in his family although he often feels misunderstood by them. He tends to be a solitary figure, always looking for the ideal partner.

Upside down

Well-loved and respected at work, he is refined, and a lover of poetry and painting. He likes to give flowers. He applies a scientific approach in the search for transcendental knowledge through reading ancient texts; his mission is to unite science and art with religion. He would like to develop his capacity as a medium through the esoteric sciences, but in an analytical way. His personality leads him to say, 'Seeing is believing'.

21   Nelchael   21

Attribute: Unique god.

Planet: Uranus.

Angelic choir: Cherubim.

Ruling hour: From 6.40 am to 7 am.

Reasons for invoking:

To destroy the power of the enemy.

To protect us against slander and also those who want to take advantage of innocents.

To help us understand astronomy, astrology, geology, mathematics and exact sciences.

22. YEIAYEL

Right way up

Whoever is born under his rule has a spirit marked by the principle of change, because he knows that nothing is permanent and that not a moment in life should be wasted. Original and exotic in thought and action, he is often seen as being mad or superstitious. He has philanthropic ideas, is generous, and cannot stand human suffering, always working for the common good. He feels the need to travel and to get to know other, mysterious countries. An excellent medium, he is consulted by people who, believing in his ability, seek happiness through his predictions and premonitions.

Upside down

Compassionate and diplomatic, he has a talent for tuning in to those around him. He is always spreading joy.

22   Yeiayel   22

Attribute: Divine justice.

Planet: Uranus.

Angelic choir: Cherubim.

Ruling hour: From 7 am to 7.20 am.

Reasons for invoking:

To protect businesses.

To protect fame and fortune.

To help with studies.

To help decide on a vocation and new paths.

23. MELAHEL

Right way up

He never turns aside from any duties. He likes everything to be absolutely correct, wants everything to be perfectly ordered. A master of communication, he expresses his feelings freely, although he can sometimes be shy or introverted on first contact. He is attracted to spiritual philosophy and he could be a visionary as he has strong premonitions. Audacious, he enjoys dangerous expeditions and exotic jobs. He is an active ecologist and an expert in healing plants.

Upside down

He has extraordinary intuition for knowing people's problems and innermost secrets, and helps resolve them with the assistance of plants. He believes that God is truly present in nature.

23   Melahel   23

Attribute: God who frees us from evil.

Planet: Uranus.

Angelic choir: Cherubim.

Ruling hour: From 7.20 am to 7.40 am.

Reasons for invoking:

For help in realising our desires.

For protection in political and public activities.

To receive abundant funds for our work.

For protection against arms and assault.

To strengthen the effect of medicinal plants.

24. HAHEUIAH

Right way up

He has a karmic connection with the country where he lives. His strong personality is characterised by dignity and respect. Blessed with great spiritual powers, maturity and judgement, he is a friend and companion who everybody wants to be around. His analytical nature looks for answers within religious concepts for all that happens in the world. A good administrator, he is blessed with natural 'luck'.

Upside down

He is concerned about people who have had problems with the law, and offers them work and financial and moral support. The safety of children and of the community also concerns him. He uses the media, radio and television to gain attention, and sometimes creates controversy in debates.

24   Haheuiah   24

Attribute: God of genuine kindness.

Planet: Uranus.

Angelic choir: Cherubim.

Ruling hour: From 7.40 am to 8 am.

Reasons for invoking:

To obtain the grace of God.

To protect prisoners, fugitives and those who suffer unjust punishment.

To protect us against car accidents and any type of violence.

25. NITHAIAH

Right way up

He possesses serenity, moderation, balance, self-control and patience, all of which help him to achieve emotional and material stability. Benevolent even towards his enemies, he leads a life of happiness and pleasure. Generally self-taught, he is well-informed on all subjects. Great paranormal powers are within his scope, and the desire to master the esoteric sciences. He knows how to turn to prayer for help with problems and attract revelations that will influence the behaviour of others.

Upside down

He loves peace, solitude, contemplation and the mysteries of nature. From childhood he has understood the meaning of things, not as an analyst but as an observer. He enjoys the strong protection of superior teachers.

25   Nithaiah   25

Attribute: God who gives wisdom.

Planet: Mars.

Angelic choir: Powers.

Ruling hour: From 8 am to 8.20 am.

Reasons for invoking:

To receive wisdom and revelations
about occult mysteries.

To use white magic in order to bring
about new revelations.

To achieve peace through knowledge of truth.

26. HAAIAH

Right way up

Just and benevolent, he is blessed with compassion and balance. He knows that earthly laws can and must be changed. He likes logical solutions and sees the word 'destiny' as a synonym for change and renewal. Working tirelessly towards realising his ideals, he enjoys travelling, and adapts easily to different climates, people and languages.

Upside down

He has access to high social and governmental circles and is a messenger of peace – a conscious collaborator of divine providence. On his transcendental mission, he restores divine order, being a secret master of white magic.

Attribute: Hidden god.

Planet: Mars.

Angelic choir: Powers.

Ruling hour: From 8.20 am to 8.40 am.

Reasons for invoking:

To help us win legal proceedings.

To uncover conspiracies.

To help us look for truth in order to
contemplate divine things.

27. YERATEL

Right way up

Intelligent, balanced and mature, of noble and refined appearance, he follows his instincts as well as the advice of others. He has high levels of initiative and perseverance and is protected against all types of negative forces. His life is clear and full of joy. He does everything lucidly and in a considered way, and his strength of action is invincible. What he starts always ends in success.

Upside down

He has the capacity to know the future through oracles, dreams or projections, and constantly updates his information. A defender of science and the arts, he is able to move great numbers of people with his ideals.

27   Yeratel   27

Attribute: God who punishes the bad.

Planet: Mars.

Angelic choir: Powers.

Ruling hour: From 8.40 am to 9 am.

Reasons for invoking:

To ask for protection against unfair attacks.

To give us knowledge of divine truths.

To succeed in business.

28. SEHEIAH

Right way up

He has great commonsense and behaves with prudence and wisdom. He faces everything with dignity and everything in his life works perfectly. Authentic and real, he always manages to emerge from the most chaotic circumstances thanks to his bright ideas. His spiritual strength is intimately linked to angels and – even without knowing it – he helps relieve human suffering. He always has a word of optimism for others, especially those who find themselves in uncertain situations, because he is always consciously or unconsciously in harmony with divine sources.

Upside down

He has premonitions regarding travel. It is wise to listen to him before undertaking a journey.

28   Seheiah   28

Attribute: God who cures illnesses.

Planet: Mars.

Angelic choir: Powers.

Ruling hour: From 9 am to 9.20 am.

Reasons for invoking:

To protect us from fires,
accidents and illness.

To protect us from evil and financial ruin.

29. REIIEL

Right way up

He is outstanding for his qualities and his zeal in spreading truth and destroying slanderous writings. His behaviour is exemplary and he loves truth, peace, justice, tradition, freedom and silence. His life is enlightened through his spirit, and he follows divine rules in accordance with his level of awareness. His existence on earth is of a highly elevated level; for example, without knowing why, he goes back to the path that he should never have left. The reward is a much better life and freedom from karmic ties.

Upside down

He must be careful not to feel guilt in relation to family problems, because everyone is evolving in a way that is about renewal. His house will be clean, tidy, and pleasingly decorated with flowers and incense.

29   Reiiel   29

Attribute: God who rescues.

Planet: Mars.

Angelic choir: Powers.

Ruling hour: From 9.20 am to 9.40 am.

Reasons for invoking:

To free us from internal enemies.

To give us inspiration in prayer.

To clearly express ourselves
in the face of adversaries.

To highlight religious feelings and meditation.

30. OMAEL

Right way up

Extremely fair-minded, he lives in harmony with his universe. He has absolute confidence in himself and is prepared to fight for his ideals. He loves animals, nature and people of great sincerity. He has a general knowledge of all areas and weighs up situations in search of an objective viewpoint.

Upside down

He is successful in carrying out many things. But he exercises his free-will when choosing his destiny.

30   Omael   30

Attribute: Patient god.

Planet: Mars.

Angelic choir: Powers.

Ruling hour: From 9.40 am to 10 am.

Reasons for invoking:

The protection of the animal kingdom.

To have patience when we are anxious.

For good relations between
parents and children.

To guide our doctor or surgeon.

31. LECABEL

Right way up

He is blessed with courage when facing the most difficult of obstacles but should be careful with his power as abusing it could be extremely detrimental to him. He has natural protection and his fortune is based on his talents. His higher self instils his lower self with a gift for studying and applying his knowledge of natural forces for the good of the community. He really appreciates old books on history and archaeology.

Upside down

He is very curious to find out about other incarnations, in order to answer his queries and understand his soul and his existence. His motto is 'a healthy mind in a healthy body' and in order to achieve this balance he can go on diets and take up sport. He loves nature and animals and enthusiastically helps in their conservation – his house could be a veritable zoo. His main characteristics are stability and great interior richness, always loving truth and order.

31   Lecabel   31

Attribute: Inspirational god.

Planet: Mars.

Angelic choir: Powers.

Ruling hour: From 10 am to 10.20 am.

Reasons for invoking:

To resolve professional issues.

To resolve very difficult problems.

To receive revelations.

32. VASAIRIAH

Right way up

He is friendly, spiritual, modest and studious, with an excellent memory and able to speak various languages with ease. During his life he experiences a little of everything and he wants everyone – regardless of race, creed or culture – to have the same opportunities. His motto is 'respect in order to be respected'. He has the gift of words. He is invincible when speaking with superiors, especially in defence of the those who are ill-favoured.

Upside down

He overcomes obstacles in life by remaining internally balanced. A warrior, he acts quickly and never goes back on his decisions. His appearance does not reflect the great responsibility that he bears in relation to his peers.

Attribute: Fair god.

Planet: Mars.

Angelic choir: Powers.

Ruling hour: From 10.20 am to 10.40 am.

Reasons for invoking:

To obtain justice.

To have a good memory and
ease of expression.

To protect against those who attack us.

33. YEHUDIAH

Right way up

He is considered the archetype of God's works, fully integrated with the angelic world. He always defends good. Understanding, kind and loving, he is well-connected and recognised by everyone. He knows how to control his interior world, adapting to reality and realising his hopes and dreams.

Upside down

He works to develop his spiritual tendencies, which are of the highest level. He is a good friend and charitable to his peers, whose way he lights with his helpful actions. He works to prevent ignorance, providing education or financial resources to this worthy cause. When choosing a partner he takes into consideration that he needs a quiet home in order to have a balanced personality.

33   Yehudiah   33

Attribute: God who knows all things.

Planet: Jupiter.

Angelic choir: Dominions.

Ruling hour: From 10.40 am to 11 am.

Reasons for invoking:

To reveal hidden situations.

To recognise traitors and
discover their plans.

To reveal to us our defects and
mistaken attitudes.

34. LEHAHIAH

Right way up

He who is born under his rule is known for his talents and actions. An inspired pacifier, he is liked by everyone. He loves to resolve problems, and is always giving advice and support. His aura of trust attracts influential people who will ask him to work for them. He is a good worker, accomplishing much. His attitude is firm, with high moral principles, goodness and hospitality, although he can be disappointed when people do not meet his expectations. He goes deeply into issues that interest him, although sometimes has to be satisfied with a superficial knowledge of many things. Profoundly emotional, he transfers to his children the love that he received from his parents.

Upside down

He is talented in artistic fields – mainly music – although as a patron rather than a performer. He has latent paranormal gifts which could be liberating. Fearing disease from dirty places and objects, he is fussy about cleanliness.

34   Lehahiah   34

Attribute: Forgiving god.

Planet: Jupiter.

Angelic choir: Dominions.

Ruling hour: From 11 am to 11.20 am.

Reasons for invoking:

To calm rage.

To understand divine laws and the
structure of the universe.

35. CHAVAKIAH

Right way up

He is a great collaborator in social wellbeing, often sacrificing personal interests for others. He loves to live in peace with everyone and to see all people reconciled. Of a practical mind, he is admired for his way of resolving problems. Paying attention to detail, he speaks in a discreet and agreeable way, never using force to make himself understood. His emotional wellbeing depends on the approval of others in social settings. His appearance does not reflect the great responsibility that he bears in relation to his peers.

Upside down

He is wealthy and helps to support issues related to medicine and spirituality. His daily work is arduous and full of new situations. He must be careful not to be too demanding or strict with himself. He has an intense aversion to extravagant attitudes or social scandals. Physically attractive, he has no problems in meeting his soulmate.

35   Chavakiah   35

Attribute: God who gives joy.

Planet: Jupiter.

Angelic choir: Dominions.

Ruling hour: From 11.20 am to 11.40 am.

Reasons for invoking:

Family reconciliations.

To be forgiven for offences.

To share out inheritances in a fair way.

To ensure a good relationship between
parents and children.

36. MENADEL

Right way up

Optimistic, independent, active and advanced, he considers honesty and truth to be highly important factors in life. He possesses a lot of willpower and is shrewd, self-confident and direct in his form of speaking. He acts with discretion and astuteness, assuming responsibility with dedication and seriousness. A perfectionist who is dedicated to work, he expects the same attitude from his colleagues. He is well-liked in his work environment but is rather easily offended and quick to criticise things that he does not like. An excellent friend and companion, he is also a passionate lover.

Upside down

He does not agree with some aspects of his religion, especially those that he feels are not useful. He is known as a prophet for his profound vision – mainly on social matters. He often only asks for help when all other resources have been exhausted.

Attribute: God deserving of admiration.

Planet: Jupiter.

Angelic choir: Dominions.

Ruling hour: From 11.40 am to 12 pm.

Reasons for invoking: To stay in work.

To keep what we have.

To find lost objects.

To protect us against slander and curses.

To receive news about people far away.

37. ANIEL

Right way up

He is well-known for his talents and for his enthusiastic and helpful astral messages. He is sometimes satirical, and has crazy and revolutionary ideas, but his achievements are meaningful. He only accepts work offers or social situations if they do not go against his spiritual ideals. His firm self-control stops him from giving in to easy temptation.

Upside down

He has a small circle of loyal, constant friends and could possibly marry young, probably choosing someone older. He fights for the good of his children, and is disappointed if they do not make the most of their opportunities. He does well in public disputes.

37. ANIEL

37   Aniel   37

Attribute: Virtuous god.

Planet: Jupiter.

Angelic choir: Dominions.

Ruling hour: From 12 pm to 12.20 pm.

Reasons for invoking:

To work towards resolving difficult situations.

To encourage harmony between different people.

To reveal the secrets of nature to us.

For inspiration in meditation.

To help us express ourselves more easily.

38. HAAMIAH

Right way up

He serves God through his high intelligence and conscience, acquired through studies, which are mainly self-taught. His wisdom will be used by God to unify people and belief systems. Strongly defending individual liberties, a concept he greatly supports, he resolves everyone's problems, using his highly developed intuition. He easily accepts things which seem surprising or incomprehensible to others.

Upside down

He feels attracted to eccentric people but hates possessiveness. He does not like to do anything on a whim or change pre-established plans. He fights alongside those who stand up to wrong-doings and defends the divine with the strongest of weapons: the truth. His mission on earth is to help spiritually elevate human beings.

38   Haamiah   38

Attribute: God who is the hope of everyone.

Planet: Jupiter.

Angelic choir: Dominion.

Ruling hour: From 12.20 pm to 12.40 pm.

Reasons for invoking:

To protect against firearms.

To discover the truth and protect
spiritual works.

39. REHAEL

Right way up

He feels altruistic love for all on earth
and considers them sons of God.
He carries out exceptional healings
with his hands and even with his mind,
as well as through prayer and positive
thoughts. His truth is eternal, fulfilling
the karmic mission of overcoming the
bad. He is always studying ways and
means for overcoming evil. He believes
in miracles and that these happen
through divine compassion.

Upside down

His optimism is contagious and he
always gets on well with everyone. He is
noble and strong and sure that people
can overcome obstacles using their
intelligence. He adores his children and
does everything to guide them in life.

39 Rehael 39

Attribute: God who takes in sinners.

Planet: Jupiter.

Angelic choir: Dominions.

Ruling hour: From 12.40 pm to 1 pm.

Reasons for invoking:

To preserve health and longevity.

To protect us from evil.

To help us see when we are acting wrongly.

To influence love between parents and children and the obedience of the young towards their elders.

40. EIAZEL

Right way up

He loves reading, the sciences and knowledge in general and has brilliant ideas and noble feelings. Thanks to his intelligence and self-confidence he excels in positions of leadership. He understands other people's problems and is willing to assist them, despite knowing that some do not deserve his help. He is careless with money but never goes without. He has an imaginative mind and a photographic memory although he doesn't always accept his own perceptions.

Upside down

His conclusions are more intuitive than logical. He travels a lot, visiting many different cities, displaying in each place his presence, the richness of his personality and the nobility of his character.

40 **Eiazel** 40

Attribute: God who gives joy.

Planet: Jupiter.

Angelic choir: Dominions.

Ruling hour: From 1 pm to 1.20 pm.

Reasons for invoking:

To free us from our internal prisons.

For comfort in times of adversity.

To protect us from enemies and vice.

To free us from panic and depression.

41. HAHAHEL

Right way up

He loves truth and fulfils his duties and obligations. His is the gift of communication, and he possesses charisma and ease of learning over a wide area, especially the esoteric. He has strong powers of concentration and wisdom in matters of discernment and judgement. His aim is harmony and to teach people how to live together with a set of beliefs that come from the heart. He feels that God has a great mission for him, which will probably begin when he finds his ideal partner as this mission must be carried out in the company of the person he loves. He wants to have children so that they can continue with the teachings of truth. He tends towards spirituality, searching for truth in the teachings of the great masters.

Upside down

He has many friends and followers of his ideas, although his points of view may conflict with those of other religions. A great transformer of the world, he will live a splendid life and be happy.

41   Hahahel   41

Attribute: God in three people
(manifested god).

Planet: The Sun.

Angelic choir: Principalities.

Ruling hour: From 1.20 pm to 1.40 pm.

Reasons for invoking:

To have strength in our evolution.

To follow the light of love.

To return to the faith of God.

To protect us from calamity.

42. MIKAEL

Right way up

He knows techniques and methods
for undertaking great ventures, and
in these his diplomacy is outstanding.
He has intense protection from his
ruling angel. Being honourable, lofty,
inspired and incorruptible, he will be the
faithful confidante of those with social,
economic or political prestige and will
collaborate fruitfully with anyone who
aims to improve society.

Upside down

He is loved by the humble and attacked
by the bad-natured and opportunistic.
His message is always that of optimism
and faith, radiating energy, confidence,
inspiration and creativity.

42   Mikael   42

Attribute: He who is as God.

Planet: The Sun.

Angelic choir: Principalities.

Ruling hour: From 1.40 pm to 2 pm.

Reasons for invoking:

To be safe on journeys.

To elicit obedience or discipline
from subordinates.

To rid people, places or objects of negativity.

To shed light on all that is obscure.

43. VEULIAH

Right way up

He tends to mix well and is therefore successful at work, receiving gratitude for services rendered. He is influential among the famous, well-known and powerful, and he gains prestige from these circles. He implements up-to-date ideas and strategic actions in order to consolidate his position.

Upside down

He acts prudently, avoiding obstacles and carefully surveying the path before taking a step. He gains much knowledge from his work. He is noble, sincere, altruistic in his relationships and takes his natural place through self-confidence and good humour, without wasting energy on personal conflict.

43   Veuliah   43

Attribute: God the dominant king.
Planet: The Sun.
Angelic choir: Principalities.
Ruling hour: From 2 pm to 2.20 pm.
Reasons for invoking:
To have inner peace and prosperity.
To destroy our internal enemies, such as fear.
To be successful in just causes.
To obtain favours from important people.
For protection and prosperity in businesses.

44. YELAIAH

Right way up

He loves travelling and learning from people he meets. He is famed for his acts of talent and courage and all his ventures end in success. He fights to keep traditions alive and researches historical facts, clarifying unclear situations of the past. He well remembers past incarnations which assists him in understanding history. Generous at work, he always gives everyone a chance. He does not permit himself to become downhearted and allows nothing to impede him from achieving his aims.

Upside down

He is sure and able, and does not risk his reputation in dubious situations. Respected and admired, he is capable of finding a solution to all problems. He shows his love in constructive ways and defends dreams related to the family, their home and their cultural values.

44   Yelaiah   44

Attribute: Eternal god.

Planet: The Sun.

Angelic choir: Principalities.

Ruling hour: From 2.20 pm to 2.40 pm.

Reasons for invoking:

For courage to face adversity.

To magistrates to be successful
in judicial proceedings.

To protect us against harm from firearms
or sharp weapons.

45. SAELIAH

Right way up

Deeply interested in cultural matters, he shares his knowledge and thoughts with those who have similar interests. He is strongly linked to everything connected to decoration and good taste. He loves animals and plants and his garden is abundant with vegetation. He will always have money and the word 'crisis' does not exist in his vocabulary.

Upside down

He studies holy writings, discovering their truths. He could have revelations working with oracles or dreams of premonition. His role on earth is to teach mankind that God exists in all creation. This angel is the representative of the angelic kingdom on earth.

45   Saeliah   45

Attribute: God who generates all things.

Planet: The Sun.

Angelic choir: Principalities.

Ruling hour: From 2.40 pm to 3 pm.

Reasons for invoking:

To be healthy and recover from illness.

To exalt the humble, especially when
they feel oppressed.

To help us in learning about arts and science
for the good of mankind, plants and animals.

46. ARIEL

Right way up

He has brilliant ideas, lofty thoughts and a strong and subtle spirit. Behaving discreetly, he is capable of resolving the most difficult problems and making the right decisions. He likes to meditate and to explore new ways of understanding the mystical for the good of mankind, using the latest technology as well as age-old methods and para-psychological techniques in his spiritual quest. He attains a high position in the community, his motto being 'Let me speak so I may understand you'.

Upside down

He represents power and mankind's search for harmony. His experience in all aspects of life leads him to success. His great intellect gives him an astral crown of gold which represents the light of his wisdom. He is never disrespectful to anyone.

46. ARIEL

46   Ariel   46

Attribute: God is my light.

Planet: The Sun.

Angelic choir: Principalities.

Ruling hour: From 3 pm to 3.20 pm.

Reasons for invoking:

To receive revelations in dreams.

To have new ideas which
light up new paths.

To thank God for the goods He has sent us.

47. ASALIAH

Right way up

Elegant, firm and with great self-control, he stands out because of his charisma. He is also sweet-natured, tender and friendly. His attitude is always based on truth, and he is completely fair and incorruptible with a heightened faith. He is extremely dynamic, living from day to day, making the most of every second in order to fulfil ideas that come to mind. He can go beyond his own powers without reaching exhaustion.

Upside down

He makes sacrifices in pursuit of his ideals. He does not like confusion, especially concerning love. Proud without being snobbish, he genuinely accepts other people's beliefs and teachings. He is always changing his form without altering the divine essence.

47. ASALIAH

47   Asaliah   47

Attribute: God who shows the truth.

Planet: The Sun.

Angelic choir: Principalities.

Ruling hour: From 3.20 pm to 3.40 pm.

Reasons for invoking:

To protect against scandal and immorality.

To reveal the truth in veiled situations and
guide towards appropriate behaviour.

To understand the divine aspects of nature.

48. MIHAEL

Right way up

Affectionate and peaceful, he loves everyone deeply and has the good of the wider community in mind at all times. He brings about social and political agreements and reconciliations, and acts as intermediary in negotiations. He defends women's rights and collaborates on community-minded ideas on health, especially the wellbeing of children. Human relationships interest him, and he studies them from the aspects of philosophy, religion, sociology and psychology.

Upside down

He strengthens relations with friends and family with words of confidence. His family help out with his projects and he could have many children. As a parent, he is demanding when it comes to study, but he is also accessible, frank and strong. His earthly mission is that of humanitarianism.

48   **Mihael**   48

Attribute: Father god who gives help.

Planet: The Sun.

Angelic choir: Principalities.

Ruling hour: From 3.40 pm to 4 pm.

Reasons for invoking:

To find peace and harmony with a partner.

To have friendship and faithfulness
in marriage.

To invoke God's help.

To open up our perceptions.

49. VEHUEL

Right way up

He stands out for his talent and virtue, and his great generosity is revealed in his aura. Well-respected, a loyal supporter of noble causes, intellectually open, he leads by the example of his good conduct. Having a well-developed sense of humour, he can make a point without seeming arrogant, and expresses himself well. Innovative, unbiased, dynamic and intelligent, he has a great capacity for forgiving the mistakes of others and always judges prudently. Marriage brings him stability and his family is united and harmonious. Physically, he looks after his appearance.

Upside down

His knowledge of the world serves as proof that life is only hard for those who do not know how to make the most of the opportunities they are given. He does not like people who do not fulfil commitments they have undertaken.

49　　　Vehuel　　　49

Attribute: Grandiose god.

Planet: Mercury.

Angelic choir: Archangels.

Ruling hour: From 4 pm to 4.20 pm.

Reasons for invoking:

To bring mental understanding.

To find comfort in setbacks.

To have divine protection in the search for moral values.

To lead us towards spiritual development.

50. DANIEL

Right way up

He is hardworking, carrying out activities with love and an intuition that can reach brilliance. He is determined and does not like anything that is not clear or well applied. Extremely patient, he is capable of accepting almost everybody but he does not accept being unfairly reproached, possibly reacting aggressively. He will not waste effort in impossible fantasies. Motivated and just, he will be a public person who can deal with any issue. He will be protected from illness.

Upside down

He discovers the reason for many social problems and convinces the community about his insights and ideas. Some of the things that happened in his childhood and teenage years could leave a mark on his life. He will be strongly attached to his children.

50   Daniel   50

Attribute: God the just.

Planet: Mercury.

Angelic choir: Archangels.

Ruling hour: From 4.20 pm to 4.40 pm.

Reasons for invoking:

To receive divine compassion.

To provide us with remedies against all evil.

To create within us new hope and joy in living.

To find the right path when we are indecisive.

51. HAHAZIAH

Right way up

He loves the sciences and has a strong interest in the properties and qualities of animals, vegetables and minerals. He is purely motivated and creative, and leads a harmonious life. He tries to understand the divine order of human structures and could take his esoteric knowledge far. Such is his prestige and authority that he could run courses and conferences.

Upside down

He is always working towards peace among people, which he regards as a way of reaching perfection. A lover of nature, he has simple tastes. At the same time, he pays attention to matters such as painting, music and creating a romantic environment. His natural poetic gift leads to many revelations through esoteric work.

51. HAHAZIAH

51   Hahaziah   51

Attribute: Veiled god.

Planet: Mercury.

Angelic choir: Archangels.

Ruling hour: From 4.40 pm to 5 pm.

Reasons for invoking:

To heal mental illness.

To reveal occult mysteries.

To raise our conscience to God.

52. IMAMIAH

Right way up

Of a strong and vigorous temperament, he bears adversity with forbearance, courage and cheerfulness. He respects people who are moral, intelligent and feeling, as he knows that these values ennoble the soul and lead to a worthwhile existence on earth. He is not afraid to work and has great manual skill; he is also an excellent decorator, intuitively arranging things in the most harmonious combinations, and using different energies to protect places against negative influences.

Upside down

Always involved in social or political issues, he inspires much confidence in others. Optimistic, expressive and prudent, he has the backing to go far, even in the international sphere. He learns from his errors and never gets carried away by his instincts.

52   Imamiah   52

Attribute: God above everything.

Planet: Mercury.

Angelic choir: Archangels.

Ruling choir: From 5 pm to 5.20 pm.

Reasons for invoking:

To give up vices and bad influences.

To be protected on journeys.

To free us from our own obsessions.

To increase financial gain from honest work.

53. NANAEL

Right way up

His light is transcendental, showing the way to innocence and truth: he could have a religious or metaphysical vocation. He is recognised for his knowledge of exact sciences. Trustworthy, he never does anything out of imprudence or self-interest, and knows how to control his instincts without limiting them. He has solid relationships and is the friend whom everyone seeks. Blessed with great affection, he lives through love and is moved by everything beautiful. He chooses the quiet life, is traditional and attaches great importance to marriage and children.

Upside down

His intelligence grows through experience rather than study. He could have health problems in childhood or adolescence, but despite his physical fragility, he has an extremely agile and fighting spirit and knows how to enjoy the good things in life.

53   Nanael   53

Attribute: God who brings about
the fall of the proud.

Planet: Mercury.

Angelic choir: Archangels.

Ruling hour: From 5.20 pm to 5.40 pm.

Reasons for invoking:

For physical and intellectual rejuvenation
through stopping negative patterns.

To gain inspiration and material
support for great feats.

54. NITHAEL

Right way up

He has a great reputation for his writings and his eloquence. Due to his merits and virtues, wide vision and foresight, he is confident in holding important positions in government or business. The personification of good, order, justice and correctness, he possesses a strong personality. He knows much about spiritual and metaphysical fields.

Upside down

From an early age different from others, he stands out for his beauty and grace in walking, dressing and speaking. His soul shines and he rules over beauty and society. Blessed with the faculties that allow him to turn anything into reality, he enthusiastically defends good against evil and is discreet when making judgements and offering spiritual guidance.

54   Nithael   54

Attribute: God of the heavens.

Planet: Mercury.

Angelic choir: Archangels.

Ruling hour: From 5.40 pm to 6 pm.

Reasons for invoking:

To help us live a long life.

To protect against danger and accidents.

To achieve stability at work and maintain
the necessary means for survival.

55. MEBAHIAH

Right way up

He stands out for his positive deeds, his kindness and his zeal in loving God and all men. He knows the path he needs to follow, understands the divine mysteries and actively promotes religious concepts. He is not attached to material things. Always available, he is at his best when working for the good of the community and with suitable companions for his life's journey. His grasp of situations and events – including the unexpected – is great, and he resolves any associated problems with creative approaches. It is important to him that his existence continues through his children.

Upside down

He has a mystic and enigmatic soul and is seen as enlightened, although he is sometimes misunderstood. He helps through healing hands, or when he is defending someone who has been unjustly treated.

55   Mebahiah   55

Attribute: Eternal god.

Planet: Mercury.

Angelic choir: Archangels.

Ruling hour: From 6 pm to 6.20 pm.

Reasons for invoking:

To increase fertility.

To protect our morale and religion.

To help us in all we need to understand.

56. POIEL

Right way up

Held in high esteem by all, due to his modesty and good humour, he is open to everything that symbolises vitality and generosity. His fortune is acquired through his skill and good behaviour. It important and logical to him that he obtains almost everything he desires, including worldly things. Recognition comes for his talents, often from far away.

Upside down

He balances reason with passion, assists others through love and without discrimination. Always optimistic, he knows how to bring out the positive qualities of people and situations, working in accordance with a spiritual and angelic philosophy. His charm lights up the life of all who approach him.

56. POIEL

56   Poiel   56

Attribute: God who holds up the universe.

Planet: Mercury.

Angelic choir: Archangels.

Ruling hour: From 6.20 pm to 6.40 pm.

Reasons for invoking:

For general good fortune.

To have success in spreading our beliefs.

To help us to meet demands.

57. NEMAMIAH

Right way up

He is tireless in his efforts to improve society and abolish the privileges or resources of people who do not deserve them. His aim is to attain a position of leadership. He stands out for his bravery and great love for truth, fighting malignant forces through reading and intellect. He is successful in his travels abroad and protected from betrayal and vengeance.

Upside down

He receives great revelations in dreams, defends good causes and is called on to make plans, being considered an excellent economist and administrator, especially in times of crisis. Positive, active and friendly, he is the centre of attention due to his personality and willpower and his passion for everything and everyone. He loves family life and his children.

57 Nemamiah 57

Attribute: Praiseworthy god.

Planet: Venus.

Angelic choir: Virtues.

Ruling hour: From 6.40 pm to 7 pm.

Reasons for invoking:

To be lucid and clear in life's actions.

To grant us prosperity in all sectors of life.

To free people from vices and lead them
to a healthy life.

To protect and guide all who work for just causes.

58. IEILAEL

Right way up

A little shy, he is distinguished by his courage and frankness, his optimism and love of truth. He receives protection directly from the planet Venus and has the positive attributes of his corresponding signs – Taurus and Libra. He makes decisions on complicated and compromising situations with clarity of expression. He displays strong affections, deep aesthetic feelings, solidity, sincerity and has the capacity to enjoy material goods and all kinds of pleasures.

Upside down

He takes risks but does not stray too far from the traditional. He has a combative spirit and finds his perfect partner in marriage. His partner complements him so that he is strengthened in the battles he has to fight.

58   Ieilael   58

Attribute: God who listens to requests.

Planet: Venus.

Angelic choir: Virtues.

Ruling hour: From 7 pm to 7.20 pm.

Reasons for invoking:

To dispel sadness.

To help in all healing processes,
especially eye problems.

To protect those who work with metals.

59. HARAEL

Right way up

He is an avid learner, wishing to be trained in all the sciences. Enormously charismatic, he stands out for his virtue, noble spirit, jovial mood and bravery. His spirituality is so deep that he is open to teachings from divine sources. He could be a healing channel, or paint channelled pictures through working with oracles. At a mature age, he unexpectedly wins or earns money he uses mainly to fulfil the mission of his earthly existence.

Upside down

He enjoys good relations with his family, and lives in harmony with his children. He particularly likes helping people who have been marginalised by society, assisting them to build themselves up again.

59   Harael   59

Attribute: God who knows all things.

Planet: Venus.

Angelic choir: Virtues.

Ruling hour: From 7.20 pm to 7.40 pm.

Reasons for invoking:

To enhance the fertility of all living things.

To find valuable objects that have been lost.

To make children co-operate with their parents.

To help those who work in stock exchanges,
archives and libraries, and also collectors.

60. MITZRAEL

Right way up

From childhood, he stands out for his great maturity and readiness to achieve success. A tireless worker, known for his talent and noble virtues, he combines the most beautiful qualities of the body and soul. He knows how to admit his mistakes as he understands that it is through experience that we grow. Always in search of his best self, his aim is to be balanced and wise. He is a tireless worker and will be able to free himself from his karma. He recognises the hand of God in each detail of nature.

Upside down

He carries out all his daily tasks at peace with his conscience. Physically and spiritually, he could be seen as a perfect symbol of what it is to be human.

60   Mitzrael   60

Attribute: God who frees the oppressed.

Planet: Venus.

Angelic choir: Virtues.

Ruling hour: From 7.40 pm to 8 pm.

Reasons for invoking:

To heal mental problems.

To solve conflicts within one's self
and with others.

To attract fidelity from subordinates.

To develop skills and virtues.

61. UMABEL

Right way up

He loves travel and honest pleasures and is loving and sensitive. Being a traditionalist, he does not adapt easily to change, and stays loyal to the values taught to him by his parents. Blessed with great intuition, he is open to everything he encounters but without necessarily becoming involved. In social and work situations, he stays true to his ideals. He appreciates ideological support and he does not like aggressive people or those who are hard to decipher. Extremely patient and can accept anything from a loved one or relative. When he does not receive affection he prefers to be alone.

Upside down

He organises his life in accordance with his conscience, which shows up clearly in his good deeds and companionship. He is happy with his position in the community, aiming to establish a filial relationship with everyone he meets and investing energy in those closest to him or in specific causes. He is looked on favourably for his balance, sweetness, friendliness and affection. His vital strength shows itself in parenthood.

61 Umabel 61

Attribute: God over everything.

Planet: Venus.

Angelic choir: Virtues.

Ruling hour: From 8 pm to 8.20 pm.

Reasons for invoking:

To live a life according to the divine laws.

To lead those who stray from the commandments to reconsider.

To maintain harmony among friends.

62. IAHHEL

Right way up

From a young age, he is sure of his own actions, and masters his nerves. A born leader, and highly evolved spiritually, he appreciates challenges and loyally fulfils all duties and obligations to himself, his family and his community. He loves peacefulness, nobility of character and solid attitudes in others, and knows how to use his energy for his own development or for the good of humanity. He is likely to think more about others than himself. Good at tactics, he looks for immediate victory, and wins nearly all battles. He enjoys sport.

Upside down

He strives for a noble, transparent and true image. He is strong enough to bear emotionally difficult situations and knows that he must persevere in order to achieve his aims. He views the people he gets to know on innumerable business and pleasure trips as experiences which enrich his internal world.

62   Iahhel   62

Attribute: God supreme.

Planet: Venus.

Angelic choir: Virtues.

Ruling hour: From 8.20 pm to 8.40 pm.

Reasons for invoking: To gain wisdom.

To bring hidden truths out into the open.

To help understanding between husband and wife.

To abandon worldly pleasures in favour of transcendental ones.

To pacify the world's violence.

63. ANNAUEL

Right way up

He has a subtle, wise and inventive spirit. An avid searcher of knowledge, he loves to read and study. Highly evolved, his conscience produces only true words and actions. He is an excellent intermediary between heaven and earth and his great enlightenment helps him understand the mysteries which exist in relationships between all things. He adapts easily to any environment and situation, never concerning himself with safety.

Upside down

His critical, symbolic and ordered intelligence will cause him problems in finding ideal companions. He believes in the maxim, 'Sound of body, sound of mind'. When he has aches and pains, he tends to cure them himself.

Attribute: Infinitely good god.

Planet: Venus.

Angelic choir: Virtues.

Ruling hour: From 8.40 pm to 9 pm.

Reasons for invoking:

To protect against accidents.

To heal illness and ensure good health.

To help us find true spirituality and wisdom.

64. MEHIEL

Right way up

His willpower in learning is outstanding. He is the centre of attention, due to his wonderful way with words. Aware of his own defects, he is tolerant and generous, understanding of everyone and always looking for the positive side of things. He will usually keep the greater share of anything, as long as this does not have a negative effect on the others involved. He is mature, has an enlightened intellect and could have a perfect body. Full of vitality, he knows how to balance reason with passion. He loves to love and to be loved, and protects his family with his strength. He finds it difficult to detect betrayal and is a little naïve in thinking that everyone is his friend. He angers quickly when treated unfairly.

Upside down

He is constantly going on journeys, and to meetings and to parties. He always thinks that things are in his favour, even when he is in difficulty. There is generally no room in his life for superstition or similar beliefs about destiny.

Attribute: God who gives life.

Planet: Venus.

Angelic choir: Virtues.

Ruling hour: From 9 pm to 9.20 pm.

Reasons for invoking:

To protect business.

To give us comfort in adversity.

To be inspired to write well.

To protect us from traffic accidents.

65. DAMABIAH

Right way up

An extremely elevated spirit, he lives his life at a deep level, and is generous and noble. He has enormous possibilities for success and financial help in his searches and expeditions. The useful discoveries he makes, which are very important to him, bring him renown. With his positive way of thinking, he could break any jinx.

Upside down

He often changes where he lives without planning anything, leaving things to happen spontaneously. He is involved in multiple romantic situations as he loves freedom and cannot stand 'prison-like' relationships. True to his ideals, he never makes anyone suffer through his selfishness or by taking advantage of the defenceless.

65. DAMABIAH

65   Damabiah   65

Attribute: God who is the source of wisdom.

Planet: The Moon.

Angelic choir: Guardians.

Ruling hour: From 9.20 pm to 9.40 pm.

Reasons for invoking:

To give us wisdom and success in business.

To protect us on sea voyages.

66. MANAKEL

Right way up

He combines the most attractive qualities of the soul and personality and is known for his positive character, friendliness and goodness. He bears problems without complaining and is an eternal fighter who is a positive stimulus for individuals and for the community as a whole. His motto is 'Come out on top', and he believes that 'the only ones who fear dying are those who do not know how to live'.

Upside down

His strong receptive and observational capacities are well developed and he applies them to all situations. He draws up optimistic and logical plans, and carries them out. He is well regarded by others but does not attempt to hide his feelings.

66   Manakel   66

Attribute: God who looks after things.

Planet: The Moon.

Angelic choir: Guardians.

Ruling hour: From 9.40 pm to 10 pm.

Reasons for invoking:

To calm rage.

To protect sleep and fight insomnia.

To give us musical and poetic inspiration.

67. EIAEL

Right way up

He is enlightened by the spirit of God. Influential and trusting, he dislikes two-faced or dishonest people. He carries out thoroughly what he has to do, and stands out in his studies and research into the esoteric sciences – especially astrology and the Kabbalah.

Upside down

He turns his dreams into projects and fulfilment, as nothing is beyond the limits of his possibilities. He likes signs of affection, and pays great attention to his family. He never acts out of self-interest or leaves a task unfinished. His health is aided by not indulging in excess and understanding that the body is the soul's temple.

Attribute: God who gives joy to men.

Planet: The Moon.

Angelic choir: Guardians.

Ruling choir: From 10 pm to 10.20 pm.

Reasons for invoking:

To intensify awareness and perception.

To find consolation in the face of adversity and injustice.

To enable us to concentrate on studying mystic philosophy and religion.

To help with emotional changes.

68. HABUIAH

Right way up

He is elegant and noble, and altruistic in his relationships, thanks to his spiritual instinct. Powerful, intelligent and capable of deep analysis, his honest conduct protects him from problems and negative influence. He is well-liked wherever he goes. Sometimes he finds that doors are closed to him, but for every closed door, there are others that will open for him. He hands his future over to God with total confidence and security.

Upside down

His sometimes helps others but he needs to harmonise relations with those who are closest to him and try not to provoke rancour. He is blessed with the protection of elements – especially those of the earth – and this is perhaps why he feels the necessity to live in the countryside. Here his intelligence can show itself, resulting in good ideas.

68. HABUIAH

68　Habuiah　68

Attribute: Generous god.

Planet: The Moon.

Angelic choir: Guardians.

Ruling hour: From 10.20 pm to 10.40 pm.

Reasons for invoking:

To have productive land.

To have children with partners.

To protect health and to possess
general healing powers.

69. ROCHEL

Right way up

Blessed with strength and energy, he acts charitably towards those closest to him, and has a great capacity for soothing the suffering of loved ones. He has a magnificently inventive mind and a strong family mission to fulfil. Blessed with strong intuition – manifested through his analytical intelligence – he is detached from impulse and from materialistic tendencies.

Upside down

He adapts easily and has a great will to learn. He is unafraid of facing testing situations, knowing that when he loses in the physical plane, he is gaining something in the spiritual.

69   Rochel   69

Attribute: All-seeing god.

Planet: The Moon.

Angelic choir: Guardians.

Ruling hour: From 10.40 pm to 11 pm.

Reasons for invoking:

To help us locate lost or stolen objects.

To influence the fame and fortune of
lawyers and magistrates.

70. GABAMIAH

Right way up

He masters all the phenomena of
nature, such as power and energy.
Highly spiritual and separating himself
from all that is not essential, he can
regenerate people, plants and animals.
He perceives everything around him
and, when necessary, immediately
enters into action. Always confident
and optimistic in his romantic, social
and professional life, he is also a little
reserved and introspective at times. His
image is one of integrity and he never
has anything to hide.

Upside down

He deeply searches for his own truth
and is a true liberal. Having a great
knowledge of cosmic organisations
and the higher aspects of angelology,
he is extremely intuitive and therefore
receives a lot of information. His
religion is truth and he is the master of
his own destiny.

70 Gabamiah 70

Attribute: God, creator of everything.

Planet: The Moon.

Angelic choir: Guardians.

Ruling hour: From 11 pm to 11.20 pm.

Reasons for invoking:

To give us confidence and optimism.

To change the patterns of our thoughts.

To help us give up drugs or alcohol.

71. HAIAIEL

Right way up

He fights against all types of injustice, knowing how to differentiate right from wrong. His upright way of thinking is shown in his behaviour. His existence is synonymous with abundance and happiness, and he feels surest of himself when he has his partner's support and that of his family, who will never be a source of problems for him.

Upside down

He works quickly, generally getting results earlier than predicted. He needs to remember that all difficult moments lead to spiritual growth. A loyal person who worries about his own life, he needs to be alone at times, although he does not want to live by himself.

71   Haiaiel   71

Attribute: Our god of the universe.

Planet: The Moon.

Angelic choir: Guardians.

Ruling hour: From 11.20 pm to 11.40 pm.

Reasons for invoking:

To have courage when facing danger.

To free us from ties with those who
want to oppress us.

To give us the feeling of peace and display
strength, bravery, skill and security in all activities.

72. MUMIAH

Right way up

He is heralded for his marvellous discoveries, including uncovering secrets of nature. Hating illusions, he unceasingly searches for truth in order to reach objective conclusions, speaking out with strength and courage against evil and injustice. He enjoys change as it renews and refreshes, and he is flexible in his way of thinking. He always helps those who need assistance to emerge from oppression or depression.

Upside down

He is blessed with a superior strength, being able to access knowledge for himself and for those who need it. He battles for his ideals and works efficiently, devoting attention to studying the laws of the universe. His words bring wealth and power and he has a profound understanding of the relationship between macro and micro views of the universe.

72. MUMIAH

72   Mumiah   72

Attribute: God who ends all things.

Planet: The Moon.

Angelic choir: Guardians.

Ruling hour: From 11.40 pm to 12 am.

Reasons for invoking:

To protect the poor and suffering.

To protect us against negative feelings of others of which we are unaware.

To help us be flexible emotionally.

To help us identify our emotional shackles.

Angelic Contact

The Bible, the Koran and other holy books contain many accounts of angels showing themselves to humans, and intervening in our affairs by guiding, protecting, inspiring, and helping. But the presence of angels in the world is not confined to the distant past, as the true-life stories in this chapter demonstrate.

Angels have a spiritual nature and a spiritual soul. They can show themselves on earth in any form they choose, including the human. As spiritual beings they possess understanding and free-will and as messengers of God's designs they can indicate events to us which have already been written in the Heavens.

The following pages contain some fascinating contemporary accounts of angelic contact, told in the words of those who actually experienced them.

A story that gives hope

Throughout our lives we are blessed with spiritual experiences, some of which are sacred and confidential, and others, although also sacred, are meant to be shared. Last summer my family had a spiritual experience that had a lasting and profound impact on us, one we feel must be shared. It's a message of love. It's a message of regaining perspective, and restoring proper balance and renewing priorities. In humility, I pray that I might, in relating this story, give you a gift that my little son, Brian, gave our family one summer day last year.

On 22 July I was en route to Washington DC for a business trip. It was all so very ordinary, until we landed in Denver for a plane change. As I collected my belongings from the overhead locker, an announcement was made for Mr Lloyd Glenn to see the United Customer Service Representative immediately. I thought nothing of it until I reached the door to leave the plane and I heard a gentleman asking every male if they were Mr Glenn. At this point I knew something was wrong and my heart sank.

When I got off the plane a solemn-faced young man came toward me and said, 'Mr Glenn, there is an emergency at your home. I do not know what the emergency is, or who is involved, but I will take you to the phone so you can call the hospital.'

My heart was now pounding, but the will to be calm took over. Woodenly, I followed this stranger to the distant telephone, where I called the number he gave me for the Mission Hospital. My call was put through to the trauma centre where I learned that my three-year-old son, Brian, had been trapped underneath the automatic garage door for several minutes, and that, when my wife had found him, he was dead. CPR had been performed by a neighbour, who is a doctor, and the paramedics had continued the treatment as Brian was transported to the hospital. By the time of my call, Brian was revived and they believed he would live, but they did not know how much damage had been done to his brain, nor to his heart. They explained that the door had completely closed on his little sternum right over his heart. He had been severely crushed.

After speaking with the medical staff, my wife sounded worried but not hysterical, and I took comfort in her calmness. The return flight seemed to last forever, but finally I arrived at the hospital six hours after the garage door had come down.

When I walked into the intensive care unit, nothing could have prepared me to see my little son laying so still on a great big bed with tubes and monitors everywhere. He was on a respirator. I glanced at my wife who stood and tried to give me a reassuring smile. It all seemed like a terrible dream. I was filled in with the details and given a guarded prognosis. Brian was going to live, and the preliminary tests indicated that his heart was OK – two miracles, by themselves. Only time would tell if his brain received any damage.

Throughout the seemingly endless hours, my wife was calm. She felt that Brian would eventually be all right. I hung on to her words and faith like a lifeline.

All that night and the next day Brian remained unconscious. It seemed like forever since I had left for my business trip the day before. Finally, at two o'clock that afternoon, our son regained consciousness and sat up uttering the most beautiful words I have ever heard spoken. He said, 'Daddy hold me', and he reached for me with his little arms.

By the next day he was pronounced as having no neurological or physical deficits, and the story of his miraculous survival spread throughout the hospital. You cannot imagine our gratitude and joy. As we took Brian home we felt a unique reverence for the life and love of our Heavenly Father that comes to those who brush death so closely.

In the days that followed there was a special spirit about our home. Our two older children were much closer to their little brother. My wife and I were much closer to each other, and all of us were very close as a whole family. Life took on a less stressful pace. Perspective seemed to be more focused, and balance much easier to gain and maintain. We felt deeply blessed. Our gratitude was truly profound.

Almost a month later to the day of the accident, Brian awoke from his afternoon nap and said, 'Sit down, mommy. I have something to tell you'. At this time in his life, Brian usually spoke in small phrases, so to say a large sentence surprised my wife. She sat down with him on his bed and he began his sacred and remarkable story.

'Do you remember when I got stuck under the garage door? Well, it was so heavy and it hurt really bad. I called to you, but you couldn't hear me. I started to cry, but then it hurt too bad. And then the birdies came.'

'The birdies?' my wife asked, puzzled.

'Yes,' he replied. 'The birdies made a whooshing sound and flew into the garage. They took care of me.'

'They did?'

'Yes,' Brian responded. 'One of the birdies came and got you. She came to tell you I got stuck under the door.'

A sweet, reverent feeling filled the room. The spirit was so strong and yet lighter than air. My wife realised that a three-year-old had no concept of death and spirits, so he was referring to the beings who came to him from beyond as 'birdies' because they were up in the air like birds that fly.

'What did the birdies look like?' she asked.

Brian answered, 'They were so beautiful. They were dressed in white, all white. Some of them had green and white. But some of them had on just white.'

'Did they say anything?'

'Yes. They told me the baby would be all right.'

'The baby?' my wife asked, confused.

And Brian explained, 'The baby laying on the garage floor.' He went on, 'You came out and opened the garage door and ran to the baby. You told the baby to stay and not leave.'

My wife nearly collapsed on hearing this, for she had indeed gone and knelt beside Brian's body and, seeing his crushed chest and unrecognisable features, knowing he was already dead, she whispered, 'Don't leave us, Brian, please stay if you can.'

As she listened to Brian telling her the words she had spoken, she realised that the spirit had left his body and was looking down from above on this little lifeless form.

'Then what happened?' she asked.

'We went on a trip,' he said, 'far, far away...'

He grew agitated trying to say the things he didn't seem to have the words for. My wife tried to calm and comfort him, and let him know it would be OK. He struggled with wanting to tell something that obviously was very important to him, but finding the words was difficult.

'We flew so fast up in the air. They're so pretty, Mom,' he added, 'and there is lots and lots of birdies.'

My wife was stunned. In her mind she felt the sweet comforting spirit envelope her even more warmly.

Brian went on to say that the 'birdies' had told him that he had to come back and tell everyone about them. He said they brought him back to the house and that a big fire truck and an ambulance were there. A man was bringing the baby out on a white bed and he tried to tell the man the baby would be OK, but the man couldn't hear him. He said 'birdies' told him he had to go with the ambulance, but they would be near him.

According to Brian, they were so pretty and so peaceful, he didn't want to come back. And then the bright light came. He said that the light was so bright and so warm, and he loved the bright light so much. Someone was in the bright light and put their arms around him, and told him, 'I love you but you have to go back. You have to play baseball, and tell everyone about the birdies.' Then the person in the bright light kissed him and waved bye-bye. Then whoosh, the big sound came and they went into the clouds.

The story went on for an hour. Brian concluded by saying, 'I have a plan, Mommy. You have a plan. Daddy has a plan. Everyone has a plan. We must all live our plan and keep our promises. The birdies help us to do that 'cause they love us so much.'

Brian taught us that 'birdies' were always with us, but we don't see them because we look with our eyes and we don't hear them because we listen with our ears.

But they are always there, you can only see them in here (he put his hand over his heart). They whisper the things to help us to do what is right because they love us so much.

In the weeks that followed, Brian often came to us and told us all, or part, of the story, again and again. Always the story remained the same. The details were never changed or out of order. A few times he added further bits of information and clarified the message he had already delivered. It never ceased to amaze us how he could tell such detail and speak beyond his ability when he spoke of his 'birdies'. Everywhere he went, he told strangers about the 'birdies'. Surprisingly, no one ever looked at him strangely when he did this. Rather, they always got a softened look on their face and smiled. He has later told us that what he calls 'birdies' are really angels, but until then he had not been able to define them exactly. Needless to say, we have not been the same ever since that day, and I pray we never will be.

The airport

I had arrived at Seville airport, but nobody was there to meet me. I had no telephone number to ring and hardly any money on me. Walking would have taken me nearly half an hour – a long distance for someone carrying two heavy suitcases. As I started to get worried, a very beautiful woman came up to me and asked, 'What's happened? Hasn't anyone come to pick you up?'

I looked at her curiously and obviously did not tell her my situation – through lack of trust. 'Well, maybe they're about to arrive,' I replied. She asked me, 'Where are you going' and this time I told her and she pointed to two men who were collecting their luggage and said, 'I heard them mention that they live there, so you could ask them for a lift.'

I said I didn't know them and that I couldn't do that. She replied that they seemed trustworthy, but I said that even so I wouldn't go with them. Then the lady approached them and asked where they were going. When they told her, she explained that I had no way of getting to my house and asked them if they could please take me. The two men came up to me and asked me where I was going. When I gave my address, they said they were going there and added that they knew my sister, who was a neighbour of theirs. When I turned to thank the lady for her help, she had disappeared.

A calming voice

On 8 September 1994, a few hours before I was to have a brain tumour operated on and with my family by my side, I suddenly heard a voice which said, 'Don't be afraid, you will not die, I am with you and everything will end well.'

I was not scared and felt that someone was protecting me. The operation was a success and now, whenever I am sad or worried, I still hear that voice that tells me not to worry because everything is going to be all right. I think it is my guardian angel.

On 7 March 1997, I went to buy food and, coming out of the shop, I heard a voice saying, 'Let him go,

Diana' and I sensed that I would have an accident. I put the bags in the boot and got into the car. Although I normally don't wear a seatbelt, this time I was inexplicably inclined to put it on. After I was driven about four kilometres, the car suddenly swerved to the left and hit a parked car.

When I came to, I heard the voice again, saying, 'Let him go, Diana.' I closed my eyes and waited in order to recover. Then I cried because I felt that someone had warned me of the danger and I hadn't taken precautions. But my story goes beyond that. My boss, my friends and my family rang me all day to find out if I was all right. When I was going home from the doctor's, I realised that I was crying and that was when I saw a cloud which resembled an angel. It followed me all the way home. I was so unsure of myself and of what I was seeing that I rang my daughter when I got home and asked her if she was seeing the same thing.

'Oh God!' she said. 'It's an angel.'

I ran to get my camera but when I began to take photographs, the image disappeared.

Unexpected angel

A few years ago my grandmother suffered from all sorts of illnesses. One day she returned home ill after having dinner with her friends. I didn't attach any importance to it, but the following day she began to complain about a strong pain in her chest which reached her back and stomach. We took her to the hospital and they carried out tests on her for a few days. We all knew that, in order for her to be treated, they had to find the cause of the illness and we began to pray.

At last, the doctors discovered that she had an aneurysm – a type of hole in the aorta which leaked onto the chest, causing pain. An operation was urgently required, but it would be a very risky one. Even so, we decided that she should be operated on and we prayed for her recovery.

The doctor had to take the x-rays to find the exact point for the needle to go into the heart. Once he examined the x-rays, he was astonished by what he saw. He quickly came to tell us that the hole still existed but that, for some reason, the haemorrhaging had been stopped. He couldn't explain the cause but asked for her to remain in hospital for two days, just to see that she didn't fall ill again. It was then that we realised that the answer lay in our prayers and that an angel had heard our pleas.

Angels on the radio

Juan Pedro was born dead. That creates an intense feeling which is difficult to explain, as you feel pain for someone who you haven't even got to know. Of course pain is a great part of the emotion but for me, this sensation was mixed with another, stronger feeling. When I looked at this child's face, I asked the Lord to make him breathe. I took the little body in my hands and cried in silence.

I remember the following events. It was the festival of the Archangel, the skies were cloudy and there was some wind. As I knew that my wife was suffering, I wanted to be with her whenever possible. During the car journey, I hardly noticed the angelical music coming from the radio.

The sweet music seemingly became louder and louder until finally it interrupted my inner thoughts, disturbing me. Irritated, I tried to turn down the volume of the radio, but it was switched off. I stopped the car and stared in astonishment and then looked all around me. I was disconcerted because music was still coming loudly from the car, but now I heard the song. I could not understand the words, but the sound was beautiful and abundant. It seemed like children's voices mixed with others which we could identify as angels.

When the music stopped, my heart had changed. I knew for sure that my son had let me into the secret: 'The place where we are destined to go is prettier than our current life.'

Miraculous birth

I was pregnant and had three scans which showed a child with multiple deformities. I could have aborted but I thought that God would give me a second opportunity. I told myself, 'If a deformed child is born, I will have to accept it. Who am I to stop its birth?' My mother would not be able to look after my child while I was at work so if I wanted this child, I would have to care for it myself.

One night, I had intense nightmares. I saw in my dreams dark elements which surrounded me and warned me of dangers, but angels also appeared to make me happy. Then I saw the devil crushing my baby and when I thought I had woken up, I saw my unmoving body. 'I am dead,' I thought, but by my side there was an angel, which gave me great joy. I called my husband and I went, with the angel, to the room next door, finding my own dead body there. I remembered in this moment, 'No, we aren't dead.' I found my body and knew I had to get up. Then I saw myself giving my baby to a young girl, while the doctors were in the room saying, 'She doesn't want it.' When I awoke and saw that it had all been a dream I decided to go ahead with it and fight for a comfortable life for my child.

The baby weighed less than two pounds but survived. I think the angel entered my dream to give me comfort and that has changed my life.

My encounter with an angel

My story with an angel happened in less than twenty-four hours. Since I know that I have an angel and that they exist, I thought I should share my experience with others.

It happened one night as I returned from the last of my Christmas shopping. I was driving on a road which has many curves and when I saw the danger I was in, I slowed down. But the rear of the car skidded in the sand and I lost control. I started to accelerate in order to get some stability and stop my car from crashing into others. I don't know exactly what I did, but my car flew into the air and flipped over several times until it landed in a field. I came to and saw the broken rear windscreen swinging in the air, just in front of my eyes.

Although the car was completely destroyed, on my side the windscreen and door window had hardly been touched. As my car had flipped over so many times, it should have been totally destroyed and the roof should have crushed me. I strongly believe that my guardian angel saved my life. It is as if I was protected by a magic bubble. When I got out of the car and the ambulance arrived, the medics couldn't believe that I was still alive. They were even more surprised when they realised I had hardly a scratch on me and that I could walk unaided and in no pain.

I am sure that there are angels out there, around us, looking after us day and night. Although I don't know exactly which one is mine, I would like to thank him for not letting me die yet.

My celestial experience

I believe in angels and I suppose it is because I grew up in very Christian surroundings. I had heard that my family had had various experiences with them but I had my first own personal experience when I was thirteen.

One night, while I was in bed, I woke up with the feeling that someone was in my room. I was scared stiff as nothing like that had ever happened to me before and the only thing I could think of doing was to call to God and ask for help, as I often did in my prayers.

I waited for the figure to disappear, but what I saw was totally unexpected. I was quite prepared to see strange things, but I could not have imagined finding an angel in my room. The figure was the most beautiful that I had seen in my life. It wasn't transparent, floating or wavy, as shown in cartoons and films. He was solid, tall, obviously strong, blonde and seemed to shine from inside.

This was not the first time I saw the angel (for what else could it be?), as about one year later I called him again to ask for protection against evil spirits. I am sure he is my guardian angel and although I hadn't seen him before, since I discovered his presence I feel safer, as I know that he will return if I need him.

Maria's angel

In summer 1995, our daughter Maria was going through a serious depression. She had been married for about a year and she was getting more and more depressed. She told me that she had even gone to the cupboard, taken out her husband's gun, loaded it and pointed it at her head, as she wanted to end her pain. Her husband, her father and I had all tried to help her, along with the doctor, but she wasn't getting any better and we thought we could lose her. All we could do was to hope and pray that she would get better.

And that was what we did until the moment when we lost hope. I begged for a sign to show me that Maria was going to get better and that sign came. It was a hot day in August and I was inside with the air-conditioning on, sitting on a stool, when a little feather fell from above and landed on my trousers. I thought that maybe it was the sign that we had been praying for and I suddenly felt a strong feeling of peace, convinced that Maria would now get better quickly. That day I asked Maria to see another doctor to check the previous diagnosis and we were surprised to hear that he had found a hormonal imbalance which he treated with medication. My daughter got better.

The feather falling was not just chance, as it happened twice more – once at the funeral of my brother's father-in-law and once in my car. I know this sign came from my angel, thanking me for having prayed so strongly. Now I often feel him very close to me and I thank God for my guardian angel.

Confirmation

My life was going pretty well. I was working for an important company, I was a lay preacher in my church and I was very active in mission events, but I wasn't happy. One night, while sleeping, I was woken up by the sound of my name. I am usually a light sleeper and when I woke up – I normally wake up quickly and ready to go out – I had the feeling that my grandmother was there, watching me. She had died about five years before and had been very active in the church when alive. I remembered that she had talked to me in dreams and left me messages to persist in my desire to be superintendent in the district. A year later, I was asked to serve in three small churches and I accepted. I have only ever received complete happiness from this work.

I remember them exactly

When I was around four years old, I went to a Christian pre-school. On my first day, the teachers let me play in the playground, although they didn't tell us that the older children played there too. Soon, the older children stopped us from playing and I slipped, lost my balance and fell headfirst into a metre-deep hole. I remember that at the bottom there were two angels waiting to pick me up and stop me coming to any harm. I had never seen them before, but I can still to this day remember exactly how they were. My parents didn't believe me but the teacher who saw me fall did. He told my parents that he saw me fall headfirst, but that I had come out completely unhurt and unscathed. That is probably why I have always believed in angels.

Ordinary people or angels?

My story starts when I was returning from visiting some friends on the beach with my girlfriend. We were driving down a road I knew very well when my car literally flew and we found ourselves thousands of miles from our destination. This – what I call 'interstate pull' – left us far away in a broken car. It was getting dark and after some minutes a 40- or 50-year-old couple turned up in a white car and offered to help.

I told them that I didn't know what to do, as the car showed no signs of working. They asked us where we were going and we told them what had happened, saying that we were lost. Without giving much importance to our story, they offered to take us to our city and we immediately accepted. On the journey, I watched them and noticed that there was something strange and shiny about them. When we arrived, they gave us their address and a few days later we sent them a card to say thank you, but it was returned to sender. I don't care if they were angels or not, but for me they were two good people who saved us from trouble when we were far from home, in a broken car and with nowhere to go.

Angels in Ravensbrück

One of the most popular angel stories of this century happened in a gruesome Nazi concentration camp in World War II, as told by Corrie Ten Boom, in *A Prisoner – And Yet*. She and her sister Betsie had just arrived at Ravensbrück, in Germany, where new prisoners were being searched. Corrie was hiding a Bible under her dress.

> It did bulge out obviously through my dress; but I prayed, 'Lord, cause now thine angels to surround me; and let them not be transparent today, for the guards must not see me'. I felt perfectly at ease. Calmly I passed the guards. Everyone was checked, from the front, the sides, the back. Not a bulge escaped the eyes of the guard. The woman just in front of me had hidden a woollen vest under her dress; it was taken from her. They let me pass, for they did not see me. Betsie, right behind me, was searched.

*But outside awaited another danger. On each side
of the door were women who looked everyone over for a
second time. They felt all over the body of each one who
passed. I knew they would not search me, for the angels
were still surrounding me. I was not even surprised when
they passed me by; but within me rose the jubilant cry,
'O Lord, if Thou dost so answer prayer, I can face even
Ravensbrück unafraid'. The proof of this is that I am
able to recount my experience.*

Angel in Manhattan

I work in Manhattan and I have a crazy timetable
– like all modern mothers. The last six months have
been very stressful for me, because I have to juggle with
work, household chores and free time. My husband
also works and he helps me out a lot, although he has
an intense work schedule. My mother lives with us and
helps me but we never have enough time or energy to
do everything. This has caused some tense moments
between me and my husband.

Here is my story about angels. I had got onto a train
and an elderly couple came up to me and said, 'We'll
sit here,' and sat opposite me. She sat down and I saw
a serious look in her face. Without saying a word, she
got up and sat in the seat behind. Her husband followed
her and sat by her side. I looked out of the window and
hardly paid them any attention. When the train started
to move she asked me, 'When the train gets going, can
we change seats? I don't like to travel backwards.'

I smiled and changed places. She thanked me and explained that they were from Michigan and that she had worked until their children were grown up. I was irritated, as it was a banal conversation which I felt no interest in. I felt that they weren't who they said they were and that her husband was very jumpy and had no interest in our conversation. He had a friendly expression but looked impatient for our conversation to finish.

She went on, 'I needed to make the most of my time. I cooked several meals on Saturday and at the weekend I did a lot of housework until late at night. At this time I complained a lot about my bad luck as I yearned for the comfortable life my parents had, but now I realise it's not good to complain so much.'

The train arrived at my station and I got up. While I was leaving, I told her I had enjoyed our conversation and she smiled and said, 'Be careful.' I walked home very slowly, thinking about the conversation we had had and, without realising, I took half an hour more than usual to get home. When I arrived, some neighbours told me that a lady had just been attacked with a knife opposite my house.

Pale, I realised that if I had gone at my normal pace and not so slowly, I would have been the victim.

Angel in the fire

One day in 1993, before going to work, I left my little daughter at my mother's house. She was two years old and very 'adventurous', as the majority of children of that age are. She went into the kitchen with my mother and stayed there while my mother left for a moment. A few seconds later, my mother called me and said that she had seen fire in the kitchen and heard a loud noise. We rushed in to look for the child and found her completely unharmed. All the kitchen cupboards were burnt black, as was the plastic chair that my daughter had sat on. She, however, was completely unscathed and calm. The stove was burnt all round and we guessed that the fire had started there.

As a believer, I am sure that it was an angel that protected my daughter that night.

Guardian angel

Our son Martin was born in November 1996. He slept in his own room from the age of four months, in a cot with two protective bars. When Martin was six months old, we heard him shout one night. My wife and I rushed into his room and found him crying on the floor. It seems he had fallen out of the back of the cot and landed on the hard floor which had no carpet on it to break his fall. My wife picked him up and after a while he stopped crying. He was unhurt. We went to the doctor and he explained that Martin hadn't suffered any harm. The next day, my wife said that she had woken up suddenly that night and heard the sound of him falling onto the floor. The only explanation we could come up with was that his guardian angel stopped him from hurting himself when he fell to the ground.

The angel and the prayer bear

When my daughter was having chemotherapy in the hospital, I went through a very bad time. I also heard many of the staff saying that they weren't sure whether Carmen would pull through, as this treatment was possibly too much for a child who was only fifteen months old.

I was working as manager of a restaurant. One day a lady came up to me and asked, 'Are you all right?'

I told her my daughter was ill but that we had faith in her recovery. The lady had a brooch in her lapel which represented an angel – so small that it was hardly noticeable, but although she wore other jewellery this stood out more than the rest. I suppose she saw me stare at the brooch and she said, 'This brooch has been in my family for generations and many people have wanted to buy it, but I don't want to get rid of it. However, I now feel that you need it much more than I do.'

She took off the brooch and gave it to me. I noticed it was very warm. After work, I went to the hospital to see Carmen. She was very pale and ill. I held the brooch for a moment without knowing where to put it, and then I stuck it in the foot of a teddy bear that she had on the bed. This bear would say 'Praise the Lord' when its foot was squeezed.

I sat down and after a few hours my little girl woke me up. She wanted her bear. This cheered me up no end as she hadn't opened her eyes for days, so I let her hug the bear. She smiled at the bear and then at me.

From that moment, she started to get better, and the bear and the angel brooch stayed on the bed. After that, she had more chemotherapy as well as radiation treatment and two operations. Her angel was always with her and I have no doubt that that angel saved her life. Today, Carmen is almost cured from a marrow transplant.

Yes, I believe in angels.

The white dog

O ne of my grandmother's old friends told me this story. My grandmother was a quiet, loving and God-loving person who always said that she'd put her hand in the fire for Him. One day, she sat on her front porch with this friend, trying to read but incapable of doing so due to her poor eyesight. She mentioned that she needed some decent lenses and suddenly a dog – white as snow – came out of the road and sat at her feet. While she looked at him, he showed my grandmother some glasses that he had in his mouth and then immediately left, never to be seen again.

Saved by an angel

M y name is Emilia, I was born in 1983 and I had my first meeting with an angel about ten years ago. My sister, two friends and I were climbing a big cedar tree where we had our 'fort'. It was in the branches, not too high but high enough for us not to be disturbed. My friends told me I wasn't brave enough to climb to the topmost branches of the tree, but I felt brave and told them I would do it. I started to climb the thick branches and noticed that they were getting nervous as I climbed higher. I stopped and looked down triumphantly. 'I'm nearly there! You'll see!', I shouted.

My sister was about to cry – maybe because she knew what could happen. Suddenly a branch broke and I fell. The fall lasted less than three seconds but my entire life passed before me in those moments. I was falling extremely quickly but I felt some arms around my waist, breaking my fall. I also heard a comforting voice in my ear, telling me that everything was all right. Although I was scared stiff, I heard this, but then I hit my chin on a branch and fell to the ground with a blow that should have at least fractured a bone. Even so, I managed to get up. They took me to hospital, where I got better.

That was ten years ago. I have never known who helped me with his arms and comforting words but I'm sure it was my guardian angel.

Two angel photos

On 5 September 1996, during Hurricane Fran, I saw what looked like an angel in the sky, and a woman – nobody I knew – took a photo. A few days later, I was queuing up for the cinema when I saw the person in front of me show a photo of the angel to a friend. It seems that the photo had been published by a newspaper and that everyone had seen it except me.

I asked if she could make me a copy, but she said that it was private, although she asked me for my phone number as she had to ask the newspaper for permission. That night, I prayed deeply to God for a photo and the next day an angel entered my dreams and told me that the photo was available and that there was another one taken on the same day. Before nightfall, I had two marvellous photos of that experience.

Tobacco and the angel

My mother – who was living with me at the time – was a very heavy smoker and spent most of the night coughing. One night the cough wouldn't let her get to sleep, and the next day she said that someone had told her, 'You are ill. Go to the doctor right now!' She looked around her but there was nobody there, although she felt a strong sense of relief in her heart after hearing those words.

She didn't understand who it had been, but she felt better than ever. She had been ill for a long time and I had been telling her to go to the doctor but she was very stubborn. She had always replied, 'I'll get better. I'll be all right soon.' However when that voice spoke to her, she changed her mind and went to see a doctor. He told her she had bronchitis and she soon gave up smoking.

My mother and the angel

My mother died on 31 December 1996 and I remember that, while she was in hospital, she spent a lot of time looking at one corner of the ceiling and smiling.

One day, instead of smiling, she frowned and I asked her why. I thought that maybe she felt she was dying, but she smiled again and told me she was seeing an angel.

The next day she had a heart attack which left her unable to speak or move for five days. On the fifth night, when I was trying to sleep in an armchair near her bed, I heard a sigh come from the bed. I got up and saw my mother moving, though still unable to talk.

Now I believe that my mother had been seeing an angel for several days and that he had come to guide her to Heaven. This apparition gave her more happiness in her final seven days than any of the doctors' medicines.

Our child's name

I was pregnant with my first child when my father – who was very ill – called us to tell us that he was dying. When we got to his house, he got up and said to my husband, 'You must call your child Francisco. That is God's desire.' I told him there was no way, to which he replied that he would be alive when his grandson was born – this being another divine design.

Feeling bad about my harshness, I explained that it could be a girl, to which he answered that it was a boy, as an angel had told him so. He also assured me that everything would be fine for us.

On our wedding anniversary, we decided to go out for dinner, and on our return I felt contractions and went directly to hospital. The birth went perfectly and it was, indeed, a beautiful boy. When it was all over, my husband rang my parents' house to say that their grandson had been born.

Sadly they told him that my father had just died. When we asked at exactly what time my father had died I found out that it was just after when my little boy was born. My father had kept his promise to stay here until then. Obviously we called him Francisco.

Touched by an angel

My name is Ana and I recently had an experience with an angel which I'd like to share, as my life has changed since then.

I was listening to the song *Touched by an Angel*, and although I knew it very well, that day I listened carefully to the words. I began to sing along and felt a sort of glow. I was standing at the window with my eyes closed, but I saw an intense, warm light that was shining towards me. The heat hit my heart and I started to cry, as I felt hurt, annoyed and in despair due to events that had recently occurred. I went on crying until a breeze brushed my face and I felt the same sensation as when my mother placed me softly in my cot, although this time I imagined it was the wings of an angel. I thanked whoever this was for this happiness and felt so inspired that I wrote a poem called *Touched by an Angel*.

Protected by my guardian angel

My husband and I had hired a rowing boat and had spent all day fishing on the lake. We had to catch the last Sunday boat home and there was a bridge that we had to cross to reach the harbour as well as a tunnel that we had to row through. We were beginning to row towards the tunnel when we stopped for a couple of minutes to pack up our fishing gear. We were a couple of metres away from the entrance to the tunnel when a motorboat, with two passengers, suddenly came roaring out of the tunnel.

Luckily there was enough space for them to get around us and avoid a crash, but if we had been in the mouth of the tunnel – which was much narrower – they would have hit us. Something – or someone – had made us stay away for an extra minute and prevented us from having a tragic accident. I think our guardian angels and the spirit of my mother protected us that day on the lake.

Thank you, my angel!

I drive a school bus. One snowy, freezing cold morning, I woke up wondering if the snow would mean that there would be no school that day. Outside, everything was slushy and dirty, but for some reason the school didn't close. When I went to work, I started to think about the children and how inconvenient it was to go to school that day. I also thought about driving more slowly, not only because the icy roads were dangerous but also to get the kids to school late in order to make up for them not being able to play in the snow at home. I always have fifteen minutes margin and normally spend it having a coffee in the petrol station. That day, other drivers told me that many roads were blocked by big branches that had frozen and snapped off the trees. Some buses were stuck out on those roads, unable to get past.

I didn't stay long, and left the petrol station behind two other buses. When I reached the turning the two other buses had taken, a fire engine overtook me very quickly.

When I reached the village, everything seemed to be in order. Then, suddenly, ice fell from one of the bridges that cross the road and it broke some high tension cables. I stopped the bus, shocked, and saw sparks flying in all directions. I didn't know what to do, but I remembered what my father always said, 'The tyres will protect you.'

Soon I felt an electric current in my hands as I drove over the wet cables and then the electricity went from the steering wheel to my metal seat, leaving me unable to drive for some seconds. The bus followed its correct path, guided by an invisible hand, and the vehicle accelerated greatly. I was out of there in no time.

Once I had recovered, I didn't remember having speeded up or having remained calm and I was sure that it was my guardian angel that had taken care of everything – and not for the first time!

Angel on the beach

It was a very hot weekend and I decided to take my children to the beach, to cool down. We were playing in the sand when an enormous wave suddenly crashed down on us and then another even bigger wave arrived. While I was still kneeling, holding my three-year-old daughter, her five-year-old sister was trying to get back to us from far away. The undercurrent of the sea meant that as she tried to come towards us she was dragged further out to sea.

I began to shout to the lifeguards, who weren't too far away, but they didn't see the emergency and carried on talking on their mobiles. A boy of around nine years old came and helped me pull her onto the sand. Once we had managed it he disappeared, although I was too busy with my daughter to realise. Soon, my older daughter coughed, spat out some water and came to.

I checked that both girls were all right and began to cry from the shock of it all. When I tried to find the boy, he had disappeared and I didn't think about him again until we were safely at home that night and I prayed to thank him. Suddenly, something inside me made me realise that the boy was really an angel. We have always been told that angels don't appear like the Bible says – with wings and dressed in white – but that they adopt different forms, often human.

The angel who looks over us

I was still living with my parents in summer 1997. My mother and I went to work in the same car in the morning and we returned together in the afternoon. We normally drove on a road where there was a lot of traffic.

On this particular day, we stopped at a pedestrian crossing. The traffic light changed and I began to move, but something stopped my car and the car next to mine. I remember thinking I had stalled, but just then a lorry came hurtling through the red light from my left, well over the 90km/h speed limit. If my guardian angel hadn't stopped my car and the car on my right, my mother and I would have been crushed. We all thanked God for stopping the engines from working.

Now that there are children with guns and knives, gangs that rule the streets, it is easier for me to send my son to school knowing that God and his angels are protecting him. It is a relief to know that when I can't be with him, God has sent his angels to protect the most precious person in my life.

The touch

In May 1990, I took my little son Daniel out of the house of a couple who were treating him badly and took him to my parents' house, where they could look after him properly. However, these weren't good times for me. I had just got divorced and I had been given custody of my child, although my ex-husband had fought for Daniel too. Luckily, my mother is the best woman in the world and she helped me fight for custody. Meanwhile, she prayed. She reminded me that God had warrior angels who would fight alongside me.

I was completely confused at this time and, as I couldn't sleep, I asked if we could all sleep together. The only room big enough was the dining room, but my mother slept on a sofa, my sister and I slept on a camp-bed and Daniel slept on a mattress on the floor. My father was very fragile at this time and remained in his room.

On that special night, we were all together and my mother read from the Bible. Then we went to sleep, although I had trouble dropping off. After a time, someone touched me on the shoulder. It was like motherly stroking. I felt it and tried to work out who was stroking me. My sister was next to me, but half-asleep, and my mother was fast asleep on the other side of the room. My son had moved a lot in his sleep and his feet were sticking out but he was also fast asleep. I was still wondering who had touched me when I asked aloud, 'Carolina, have you been touching my shoulder?' Half asleep, she said that she hadn't.

'Mum! Have you just touched my shoulder?'

'No, it wasn't me,' she replied.

'Well, someone touched my shoulder and I haven't made it up. It was a hand! It was warm and solid. A strong hand,' I insisted. My mother, of course, found the answer. She said it was an angel that had come to tell me that everything would be all right.

Now, nearly eight years later, I still think about that stroking and I do it to myself to remind myself of that feeling. Obviously it doesn't have the same effect, as I remember the touch of the angel being quite special.

If you are wondering if there was a happy ending to my divorce and the custody of Daniel, then I must say yes. In 1996 I remarried and we are now a very happy family.

A meeting

I am seventeen years old and live in the suburbs. One day, when going to the market with my aunt, I felt very hungry and we decided to stop and eat in a fast food joint. There, in the corner, I saw a man drinking coffee. He looked homeless, with a dirty beard and torn clothes. Soon he felt my look and got a little nervous and scared. I went up to him and asked him if he wanted some money, but he said he didn't need any money or food – not in a hostile way, but in a kind way.

I sat next to him as he seemed more pleased with the conversation than with material help. I told him I wanted to help him if he needed help and, to my surprise, he started to quote from the Bible about the need to not be a hypocrite and to not feel proud of giving charity or to draw attention to it. He said I should think more humbly and discreetly in order to really contribute something.

Confused, I thanked him for his vision and advice concerning charity. I went back to my table and spent a couple of minutes watching him. It was then that I realised something special.

Maybe he was someone sent by God to help people understand his message. Or an angel. Although I saw myself as a humble person until then, I am still surprised to see that someone who has been so broken and rejected by society could have been able to know my defects and show me how to really walk proudly in life.

A roomful of angels

My mother was getting gradually worse. Her breathing wasn't deep, her legs were black from the knees down and her eyes stared. She needed an operation.

She was 79, had nine children and she, in turn, was the oldest of nine children too. I was 30 years younger and lived almost next door, so I visited her very often. She was 49 when I was born, so she was never that healthy, not only because of her age but because of her brothers and sisters and the money not being enough.

She was active, always gardening, working with dad and going shopping with him. She liked travelling and telling stories. She believed in God, even though she had lost three children – one aged nine months, who died of mumps, one aged 26, who had been paralysed from the waist down for eleven years after an accident at school, and one who drowned in a river, aged 19. She was aware of what it meant to suffer and she knew that God saw her.

We were all in the hospital, waiting, hoping for the operation to be over. I told my husband that I wanted to go to the hospital chapel. We both prayed and then, suddenly, I said I wanted to go home to be with my son. He looked at me as if to ask why and at that moment the door opened. It was a nurse, who told us that mum had died during the operation.

I walked towards the ward and a moderate heat inexplicably surrounded me. When I arrived, I found a peaceful atmosphere and my mother surrounded by angels.

I have never doubted this vision and I never will. I felt the angels around me as if they were waiting for something. They took my mother and carried her to God and in that moment I heard, inside me, a message from Him which assured me that she wouldn't be alone.

The next day I went to see the priest and I told him everything – the good and bad news. The bad news was that my mother had died and the good news was that I had seen the angels of God take her.

This is a true story – maybe a sad one, but it really happened.

My son, my angel

Last year I was pregnant with my first baby and both my husband and I were euphoric about the arrival of our baby. We were trying to buy a new house and we were working very, very hard to achieve our goals – like most couples do. We were so happy with the pregnancy that we decided to let the sex of the baby be a surprise. Everyone told us it would be a girl, based on traditional ideas about pregnancy. In the fifth month, I had a dream in which a pair of blue little boots appeared and I woke up convinced that it would be a boy. I decided he would be called Ricardo. My father bet us it would be a girl but he obviously lost.

At this time, I was having a lot of problems with some of my family, especially my sister and my mother. We had argued over who would be the godparents at my son's baptism and we hadn't reached an agreement since I had fallen pregnant.

In the first week of my seventh month I started to feel bad. It was night-time and my husband was sleeping. I was feeling worse and worse so I went to have a shower in the hope that that would help. When I got out of the bathroom, my husband was awake and he asked me what was happening, just as I started to feel dizzy. He turned on the light and told me I didn't look well. We decided to go to hospital as it was Friday evening and we didn't want to wait until Monday. The odd thing is that I didn't feel bad enough to go to hospital, only a little strange. When we got there, I must have looked worse than I felt, as they rushed me into casualty.

The nurses called my doctor and they began to do tests. The foetal monitor showed a strong heartbeat, which was obviously my main concern. After more tests, the doctors discovered I had septicaemia – an infection of the blood. The problem was that this infection could affect the heart and kill me in less than two days. They found that the baby had the same infection and that I had been leaking amniotic liquid for three weeks, which they now detected in my urine. After being analysed by several doctors, they all agreed that the only way to save my life was to bring on labour, although the child would only have a five per cent chance of surviving. The outcome for both lives was unknown. While my husband wanted me to survive, I wanted to save my baby.

My parents, sister and close friends were all there by this time. They all tried to convince me to have the birth induced but I steadfastly refused. I was prepared to die so that my son could live. Then my heart suddenly stopped. All I remember is a vision of what we consider to be my guardian angel, standing with his beautiful wings open and surrounded by a shining light which warmed me and my child. My husband told me that I came back to life and that the baby was born shortly after, although he only lived a few minutes. I put out my hand and asked the nurse to give me my son and she asked me how I knew it was a boy. I told her an angel had told me so and that I had to let him go to heaven as his aim in life had been fulfilled.

For days and weeks afterwards, I was severely anaemic and depressed and I tried to work out what type of sad test I had been handed by fate. Now I believe that Ricardo's aim was to bring new peace to my life and I think he has managed it. My sister and I get on much better and my parents have been visiting me frequently for months now.

My husband and I get on better than before and we think that the angel brought us peace. Now I have had a dream in which I am pregnant again and I have to take it as a message that it will be so.

I saw my angel

I had been praying to Jesus for two or three years for him to let me see an angel. I was very worked up about the idea and couldn't wait for the moment to come. Would the meeting happen in the street? Would a human figure call at my door? The days went by and little by little I started to feel disappointed. I concluded that Jesus didn't want me to see one, and given that everything depends on Him, I couldn't do anything. One day I went into the bathroom and sat down. I thought about how little I could do about my dream of seeing an angel not being granted. I stared into the mirror while I thought and then I saw an angel! It came out of the wall and its face came very close to mine. Amazed, I saw its intense eyes looking at me. We stared at each other for a few moments and then the angel went away.

I couldn't say if the angel was a man or a woman, but I believe that isn't important. It wore a long tunic with a veil over its head and the veil was folded. It was completely calm and I will never forget the intense look of love and those black eyes which represented peace and happiness.

Angels around me

One summer afternoon, thunder followed by lightning surprised me in my house. I was peeling potatoes and watching the storm from the kitchen

window, from where I could also see the spire of the
church. While I was watching, I saw a bolt of lightning
hit the bell tower, and I rang a friend so that he could
warn the vicar while I rang the fire-fighters. Then I ran
to the church.

I was the first to arrive and I saw flames coming out
of the windows, starting to reach the church roof. I went
in through the back doors and ran to the sanctuary. It
was full of smoke, and chunks of burning ceiling were
falling to the floor and quickly setting fire to the carpet.
At the back of the church I found relics which I picked
up before leaving. At this moment the vicar and some
parishioners arrived. The firemen acted quickly and
cleared the area. I was worried for the big, tin cross, the
Bible and the vicar's study book on the altar. I couldn't
let those precious things be destroyed. Although the
firemen had got us all out of there, I ran barefoot to try
and rescue these things.

I put the very heavy Bible under one arm and the
even heavier cross under the other and tried to go to a
safe place, but I couldn't move. I felt like someone was
pushing me back, stopping my feet from moving. I could
see the vicar and the firemen telling me to get out of
there but I couldn't move. Then a chunk of ceiling fell
right in front of me. The flames started to envelope me
and I had to move away. I jumped onto the fallen roof,
even with my heavy load, and ran down to where the
others were. I arrived crying and retching, but happy to
have recovered the most precious parts of the church.

The following Sunday, we held mass outside the
church. The vicar sang a song that he had written about
the fire which had consumed our church, talking of the

274 THE POWER OF THE ANGELS

saints and angels that had helped me and enabled me to recover those artefacts. It was the most beautiful song I had ever heard, although I said it wasn't necessary. He insisted again that the song was dedicated especially to the angels and me, as all of us were part of the miracle.

Then he explained that he had seen angels all around me while I carried the cross and the Bible. He said that two angels held my legs while another two held my arms to stop me running. He also said he saw them shielding me from the flames. Then two angels literally lifted me by the arms and they all carried me to safety. I didn't see the angels but I felt their presence.

After the church had been restored, the vicar gave me his Bible as a study gift. Twenty years have now gone by and the vicar has continued in his ministry there and I have continued in my work. My Bible and I have fought to stop people going to hell, and although I still haven't seen my guardian angel, I see his work and know he is there, looking after my family and myself.

Protection from danger

When I was twelve, my parents went out one afternoon and left me to look after my six-year-old brother. Just after they'd gone, a storm started and my brother, who was looking out of the window, said there was an evil spirit in the house. I don't know if it was a trick of my mind which made me see it, but as I looked in that direction I saw an ethereal figure walking around the house. However, I wasn't scared

and neither was my brother. We went out together and
it suddenly stopped raining and the wind died down.
The figure I saw had brown hair and was tall and
strong, was white, and bore a remarkable resemblance
to Jesus, although he could have been an angel. In the
teachings at school, they talked a lot about angels, so
I was familiar with them. After about an hour, we went
into the house again and went to bed.

When my parents arrived home, they woke me up
and asked if I had been playing with matches. I said
I hadn't, but I didn't tell them about the vision we had
had. My father was still angry and told me he had seen
a wax figure with pins in it in the cupboard with signs
of having been burnt. I explained that I didn't know
what had happened and then I told them my story, but
they didn't believe me.

The next day, I went to visit a friend and I told him
the story, but he didn't believe me either and laughed.
I forgot about the conversation and the angel until, one
day, my brother reminded me of it and told me what
he remembered. Now he is sure that there is always
someone around us, protecting us, although I don't
know if it is an angel or a spirit.

Angelic Glossary

This glossary explains some words and terms related to angels in the context of Christianity and other major religions.

Agnosticism

This word comes from the Greek *a* (denial) and *gnosis* (knowledge). Agnosticism is the view that nothing is known of the existence of God nor is likely to be.

Angel

The word angel comes from the Greek for 'messenger'. The Jewish and Christian religions and Islam all recognise the existence and role of angels, as do some other faiths.

Angels are spiritually created beings, immortal, innumerable and invisible. Their purpose is to worship God and to execute His will, and among their tasks is the guidance, protection and comforting of people on earth. Fallen angels are those angels who rebelled against God and became evil. Chief among the fallen angels is Satan.

The Antichrist

The name Antichrist was applied by the early Christians to any rival or enemy of Christ, who they expected to return before the end of the world.

Atheism

This term comes from the Greek *a* (denial) and *theos* (God). Atheism is disbelief in the existence of God in any form. Like agnostics, atheists are materialists for whom the physical universe is all that exists. Many people over the centuries have been inappropriately called atheist because they did not accept popular beliefs of the time; for example, the Romans considered the early Christians atheists because they didn't recognise their gods.

Baptism

This word comes from the Greek *baptiso* (submerge). Baptism is an immersion of the body in water or a sprinkling (of holy water) to symbolise identification with a belief or cause.

Water has been used for thousands of years as a symbol of purification in many religions. In the ancient world, the waters of the Ganges in India, the Euphrates in Babylon and the Nile in Egypt were regarded as holy, and people bathed in them to purify themselves. In Christianity, the sacrament of baptism signifies purification in the name of Christ and admission to the Church, accompanied for babies by name-giving.

Blasphemy

Blasphemy is irreverent, negative or profane talk about God or holy matters, and many religions consider it a sin. A number of slang words and expressions in common use today were in the past considered blasphemous.

Christ

The word Christ comes from the Greek *kristos* and is a title, equivalent to the Hebrew term *messiah*, which means 'the anointed'. Historically, Christ as a title was not only used for priests who acted as intermediaries between God and humanity but also for certain kings who were viewed as representatives of God and thus acquired priestly dignity. Later, the term was applied to the prophets and the patriarchs of the Old Testament. Gradually, however, Christ came to be reserved for the redeemer and restorer of the Jewish nation and is now used exclusively to refer to Jesus, as the anointed one who frees us from sin.

As Christ, Messiah or The Anointed, Jesus has three positions: prophet, priest and king. As prophet, He spreads the word of God and is His representative before man. As priest, Jesus represents man before God and restores communion between both, as He has offered himself as the sacrifice for the sins of mankind. As king, He rules over His people and is present among them when they gather in His name.

Christian

The word Christian comes from the Greek *kristianos*, which, in turn, comes from *kristos*, 'Christ' or 'anointed'. As such, a Christian is a follower of Jesus Christ, although the word is also used as a synonym of 'disciple'. The New Testament states, 'The disciples were called Christians first at Antioch' (*Acts 11: 26*). In this Syrian city, there was a very dynamic church, founded by Christian Hebrews from Jerusalem and strengthened by the sermons of Paul and Barnabas, who later became missionaries.

Church

This term is used in two ways – the visible church and the invisible church. The former is composed of those currently living who claim to be believers and who congregate to worship God. The invisible church is the body made up of those who are truly saved – a composition only known by God, as humans cannot see inside the hearts of others. The real Church of God is not an earthly organisation with people and buildings, but a supernatural entity made up of believers, which covers the entire period of existence of mankind on earth and all the people who have been called to it.

Communion

The Greek term for communion is *koinonia*. In the Christian Church, the participation of the faithful in spiritual acts as members of one body, especially in the supper of the Lord or the Eucharist, is known as communion. Real communion among people implies sharing of interests, desires, motivation, emotions and common objectives.

Condemnation

This can refer to both the act of declaring a person who acted wrongly guilty and the punishment consequently inflicted upon him or her.

According to Christian doctrine, without Jesus we would all be condemned by God, not only for Adam's sin but also for our own. Christians escape condemnation as they are pardoned by Christ, although they are still required to live good and faithful lives.

Creation

This expression refers to everything that exists, with the exception of God Himself. From ancient times, all cultures have had their own versions of the origins of the universe. The Bible tells us that God separated light from darkness, day from night, and created all that is on the earth, including men and women, plants and animals. As humans, we cannot create in the same way as God created (that is to say, forming everything that exists out of nothing) and we cannot even save ourselves.

Death

The word 'death' is used in two main ways in the texts of the Bible. Firstly, it is used to describe the end of physical life and, secondly, it is used to refer to those who are lost. In this latter sense it means eternal separation from God as a result of sin, in a conscious state of damnation without hope of liberation.

Death is not natural to human beings as, when God created Adam and Eve, death was not part of the created order. It was not until they sinned that death became part of the fate of humanity. The Bible tells us that death will be destroyed when Christ returns.

Faith

As used in the Bible, the word 'faith' (from the Latin *fides*, meaning 'believe', 'trust')' has two main meanings. In the first, it is the synonym of firm trust: 'Now faith is being sure of what we hope for and certain of what we do not see'. As such, it is a gift of God and comes from hearing the divine word. Faith is the means through which the grace of God is granted to the believer who trusts in Jesus. Without faith, it is impossible to give thanks to God. In the second sense, faith refers to the doctrine or collection of truths that make up the Christian and other faiths.

St Paul stated that a sinner cannot reach salvation through good deeds alone but also needs to have faith in the free grace of God. According to this belief, which was supported by Martin Luther during the Reformation, good deeds are a consequence of faith.

Glorification

This is a state of pure exaltation and perfection. One of the tasks of the angels is to glorify God. Christians believe that those who have died will be glorified in resurrection and that believers who are alive when the Lord returns will be instantly glorified. Glorified believers will have an incorruptible body and not have a sinful nature, nor be subject to death.

God

G od is the supreme being, creator, bearer and sovereign of the universe. He is the only creator or source of all things that exist and is described in terms of perfect attributes; for example, his infinity, immutableness, eternity, goodness, knowledge (omniscience) and power (omnipotence). Most religions ascribe to God (or His equivalent) certain features of character such as will, love, anger and compassion.

Also known as Jehovah or Yahve, the Christian God lives eternally in three 'personages': the Father, the Son and the Holy Ghost. Jesus gave Him the title of Father, which refers more to His love and care than to His power. Jesus, known as Christ, was understood to be the Son incarnate or the divine Word.

Gospel

T he term gospel comes from Latin and means 'good news'; it refers to the first four books of the New Testament which record Jesus' life and teachings. These books were written by Matthew, Mark, Luke and John, who are known as the evangelists, a word which comes from the Greek and also means 'good news'.

St Paul refers to the gospels in 1 Corinthians 15: 1–4 when he writes: 'Now, brothers, I want to remind you of the gospel I preached to you, which you received and on which you have taken your stand. By this gospel you are saved, if you hold firmly to the word I preached to you.'

Grace

Grace can be defined as 'undeserved favour', which is granted without merit on the part of the receiver. The grace of God is His free-will which both benefits creation in general (common grace or providence) and gives salvation to believers (special grace). Grace is different from justice and compassion: justice is receiving what one deserves and compassion may or may not be deserved. Through saving grace, we receive eternal life – something which we obviously do not deserve. However, through the love of God manifested in Jesus crucified, we receive the blessing of redemption.

Heresy

In Christian writings, this term is used in the negative meaning of a belief or opinion opposed to the doctrine of the Church. The term comes from the Greek word *hairesis*, meaning 'own choice', as in someone choosing which parts of Biblical teachings to believe and which ones to reject.

There are numerous historical heresies related to Christianity. Some of the main ones have been to deny the divinity of Jesus Christ and the personal nature of the Holy Ghost, to state that men can become gods and that there is more than one God, that Jesus lost his divinity in Hell and ended his work of atonement there, and that salvation requires only good deeds.

The Holy Ghost

The Holy Ghost, also known as the Spirit of God, the Holy Spirit, the Helper and the Eternal Spirit, is the third Person of the Trinity and thus God. He has the power to know things – even the most profound mysteries – which He reveals to believers, and is considered as the sanctifier who leads and guides us to the Church.

The Holy Ghost is represented in the Scriptures as a dove (symbolising peace and reconciliation), a whirlwind (symbolising strength), and tongues of fire (symbolising the ecstasy of believers).

Idolatry

An idol is a representation of something in heaven or on earth which is honoured and worshipped for itself. In the wider sense, according to the Bible, idolatry does not require a material image or a belief system, it can be anything that takes the place of something belonging only to God.

Idolatry is prohibited in the Ten Commandments. The influence of Egyptian and Babylonian cultures had led to the acceptance of idol worship by the nation of Palestine, until the teachings of Hebrew prophets forced the total abandonment of idols. Islam prohibits the depiction or representation of God, whether it be for worship or not. In Christianity, veneration is limited to images which show the divinity of God.

Incarnation

The incarnation, or union of divine form with human form in Jesus Christ, is a central doctrine of Christianity. The doctrine of incarnation is based on Biblical passages from John 1: 14: 'The Word became flesh and made his dwelling amongst us'. Incarnation is the act by which God, without ceasing to be God, turned into man.

Jesus – God and man at the same time – died on the cross to atone for the sins of the world and is now in Heaven as a mediator between God and ourselves.

Jesus

Jesus Christ is one of the most influential people in human history. According to the gospels, He was born in Bethlehem, in Judea, probably between 7 and 4 BC. He grew up in Nazareth, in Galilee, and when He was around 30 years old He was baptised by John the Baptist. Jesus called together twelve followers, known as disciples, and over the next three years predicted the coming of the Kingdom of God, carrying out many miracles to show that He was who He claimed to be – the Messiah or God's Anointed.

Betrayed by one of His disciples, Jesus was falsely accused of blasphemy and crucified under the decree of Pontius Pilate, procurator of Judea. He was resurrected three days later and presented himself to the disciples, telling them of the Kingdom of God and encouraging them to write the gospels for all mankind. Then he ascended to Heaven, from where He will return to judge the living and the dead.

Man

Mankind was created by God and made in His own image and, as such, reflects something of the character of God. The first man, Adam, and the first woman, Eve, were made in the image of God and placed in the Garden of Eden with the aim of being in communion with God and to fulfil the plan of God for the creation.

When Adam and Eve sinned, all humanity fell, and were condemned to die. As such, we are by nature 'children of rage' and exposed to God's rightful justice. As this is man's natural state, it is impossible for us to achieve salvation for ourselves.

Messiah

This is a translation of the Hebrew word meaning 'the anointed'. In the Greek version of the Hebrew Bible this term is translated as *kristos*, from which comes the word Christ. His arrival long heralded in the Old Testament, Jesus is regarded by Christians as the Messiah, although Jews believe that the Messiah is still to come.

According to the first three gospels, Jesus' identity as the Messiah was proclaimed by the angels in the moment of his conception, at his birth and at his baptism. The Gospel of St Mark tells how Jesus was crucified for having admitted to being the Messiah. Jesus, as the Messiah, was anointed by God to carry out a triple ministry of prophet, priest and king, freeing believers from the chains of sin and giving them eternal life.

Miracle

From the Latin *mirari*, 'to admire', miracle is the term used to describe something that seems to transcend human powers and the laws of nature, appearing to be the outcome of divine intervention or supernatural forces. For believers, a miracle is seen as God's direct and extraordinary intervention on earth. Examples from the Bible include the separation of the waters of the Red Sea, Jesus walking on water, and the resurrection of the dead.

The Bible also tells us of satanic powers capable of realising 'deceitful miracles', which, rather than encouraging people to glorify God, aim to trick them into following Satan instead.

Omnipresence

Omnipresence is an attribute which is exclusive to God. It is the quality of being present in all places, at all times. God is not limited either by space or by time, which are His creations.

Omniscience

Omniscience is another attribute exclusive to God. It is the quality of knowing everything. God knows everything that has been, that is and that will be. The attributes of omniscience, omnipotence (meaning infinite power) and omnipresence represent the nature of God with respect to His relation with the order that He created.

Oracles

Oracles are the divine inspiration or revelations given to the people by God. The means of communication can vary from dreams and visions to wisdom. The word oracle (from the Latin 'to speak') literally refers to the place where gods – such as those of the ancient Greeks at Delphi – were consulted for advice and prophecy.

Prophet

A prophet is a mediator between God and man, a proclaimer of God's Word, which they have received directly from Him.

The four great prophets of the Old Testament are Isaiah, Jeremiah, Ezekiel and Daniel, and the twelve lesser are Hosea, Joel, Amos, Obadiah, Jonah, Micah, Nahum, Habakkuk, Zephaniah, Haggai, Zachariah and Malachi.

The prophecies of the Old Testament can be classified in three categories: those concerning the destiny of Israel and the pagan nations, those concerning the coming of Christ, and those concerning the end of time.

Resurrection

Resurrection means returning to life, being lifted alive from among the dead. The word is used in different contexts in the Bible. For example, Lazarus was resurrected, which means that, like other resurrections described in the scriptures, his mortal body was invigorated and restored to the same corruptible condition as before death. These resurrections are different from the Resurrection of Jesus Christ whose resurrected body was incorruptible. For this reason Jesus is known as 'the firstborn of the dead'.

Scriptures

The word scripture is derived from the Latin meaning 'to write'. A scripture can be any religious writing; for Christians, the term Holy Scriptures is a synonym for the Bible, referring to the 39 books of the Old Testament and the 29 books of the New Testament. This latter includes the four gospels, the Acts of the apostles (which is the story of the early Christian times), the Epistles, or letters, of St Paul and other followers of Jesus, and the Apocalypse or Book of Revelations.

The word Bible comes to Latin from the Greek *biblia*, meaning 'books'. It is the diminutive form of *byblos*, which was the name given to papyrus, or paper, exported from the old Phoenician port of Biblos.

Son of God

In the Old Testament, this term refers figuratively to Israel. The New Testament uses 'Son of God' only in reference to Jesus Christ. It implies His divinity, as the title puts him on the same footing as God.

Index

A

R

S